MW01033205

Fourth Edition

This book is dedicated to all the pioneers
who overcame the toughest times and built one of
the greatest nations of all.

Special thanks to all the authors for making this book possible:

S. Patrick

Susan Morrow

Erik Bainbridge

M. Taylor

Theresa Anne DeMario

Lex Rooker

S. Walter

Shannon Azares

M. Searson

Fergus Mason

G. Arminius

M. Richard

Jimmy Neil

James Walton

P. Vlad

Edited and copyrighted by Claude Davis

(www.askaprepper.com**)**

ISBN: 978-0-692-11197-0

© 2021 Claude Davis

Fourth Edition

(a Global Brother production)

This book is in copyright. Subject to statutory exception and to the provision of relevant collective licensing agreements, no reproduction of any part may take place without the written permission of the editor.

DISCLAIMER

This book is designed only to provide information. This information is provided and sold with the knowledge that the publisher, editor, and authors do not offer any legal or other professional advice. In the case of a need for any such expertise, consult with the appropriate professional.

This book does not contain all information available on the subject.

This book has not been created to be specific to any individual's or organization's situation or needs. Every effort has been made to make this book as accurate as possible. However, there may be typographical and/or content errors. Therefore, this book should serve only as a general guide and not as the ultimate source of subject information.

The authors, editor, and publisher shall have no liability or responsibility to any person or entity regarding any loss or damage incurred, or alleged to have incurred, directly or indirectly, by the information contained in this book. You hereby agree to be bound by this disclaimer, or you may return this book within the guarantee time period for a full refund.

Some products described in this book do not comply with FDA, USDA, or FSIS regulations or local health codes. Dehydrating meat products does not reduce the health risks associated with meat contaminated with Salmonella and/or E. coli O157H7.

The instructions provided have not been reviewed, tested, or approved by any official testing body or government agency.

The authors and editor of this book make no warranty of any kind, expressed or implied, regarding the safety of the final products or the methods used. The use, making, or consumption of any products described in this book will be done at your own risk.

Some names and identifying details have been changed to protect the privacy of individuals.

TABLE OF CONTENTS

THE MOST IMPORTANT THING

My parents were pretty old when I was born, and my nana and granddad were born in the latter half of the 19th century. Consequently, I grew up "old fashioned."

The tales my parents and grandparents told me were of times that were very different. They told me of a time when you made the most of what you had, no matter how little that was. My mother would tell me of how it was common for richer families to pass down clothes to those poorer children in the community—and the children were thrilled with their "new" clothes.

My younger brother and I would come home from school to my grandparents' house, where we'd be fed soup made using the previous day's leftovers and bones the butcher was throwing out; it was the best soup I have ever tasted. My parents and grandparents were not only from a different age but also from a different philosophy.

Here we are, human beings in the 21st century, several lifetimes and a world away from our grandparents and their ways. Have we become better at living? Has modern technology given us a better world to live in than our grandparents had? I think not.

I watch as we become ever more expectant that the world owes us a living. Consumerism has reached epic proportions; people feel aggrieved if they don't own the latest gadget and struggle to cope without the Internet, unable to entertain themselves.

I find it ironic that we talk about the Internet "connecting the world." The Internet of Things, or the IoT as it's known, is the latest buzzword, where the excitement levels about interconnectivity between human operators and devices are at dizzying levels. The truth is we have never been so disconnected from life, from the world, from the soil, from the trees and other animals, and from our souls.

We have lost the power to look after our loved ones and ourselves. We are so reliant on others, often faceless corporations, to address our every waking need that many of us can barely cook a decent meal—we resort to take-out and frozen meals. Our health, both mental and physical, is suffering too because of our child-like dependence on others.

Humans need to connect again—connect to each other and connect to our world. We need to learn the skills of our grandparents, skills that allowed them and their children to survive wars and famines.

One of the most noticeable changes between our grandparents and us is that of our attitudes and expectations. Our grandparents' generation did not have the luxuries we all indulge ourselves in— luxuries that have a finite life as we take more and more from the planet.

My nana did not go out and buy wardrobes full of clothes. She would make her own clothes. She would buy the fabric, often creating her own pattern from existing clothes, cut the material, and sew the outfit. She was an amazing knitter and crocheted for the extended family.

If an item of clothing became worn or ripped or a hole opened in a sock, it would be mended, not thrown out. This was long before recycling and upcycling were seen as "on trend." This wasn't recycling; this was an expected way of doing things.

My granddad grew fruit and vegetables and fished in the river; without those home-produced foods, my mother and her siblings would not have eaten so well. He'd also barter and swap various items for meat, which was a treat for the family rather than a daily expectation as meat is now.

Home medicine was common. You simply couldn't afford to see the doctor, and so various "folk medicine" recipes were used for general illnesses and injuries. Medicines like poultices and various teas were used to treat everything from minor cuts to stomach pains. As our antibiotics stop working, we may find these home remedies useful again.

These skills were passed down. My mother, in turn, was taught from early childhood to sew and knit, making it her living as she grew into adulthood. The recipes for folk medicines and which berries were okay to eat were learned from childhood, and children really could fend for themselves.

We need to find that part of ourselves again, that willingness to stand up for ourselves and our family and say, "I'll look after you. I don't need things that don't help me survive, and I don't need objects for the sake of having them. I do need strength and health and happiness and companionship. I do need the knowledge that my grandparents had to 'make do and mend.'"

To cook and grow, build and learn. To produce but know when to stop producing. To have enough but not too much.

As a species, we are reaching a tipping point. There are seven billion of us on this small blue planet, with around 1 million more people being added every 4.8 days.[1] Our world is changing, and we have entered an era termed the Anthropocene[2], where the planetary conditions and the wilderness are being profoundly changed by human beings.

We may well find that in the coming years, those old skills used by our grandparents suddenly become needed again. The next major crisis, EMP, war, or any major disaster that you can think of will teach us the hard way. Many of us will die because so many of us are so detached from the real life.

We will find ourselves needing to replace social media with community spirit, and instead of buying objects and clothes we don't need, we will develop the "make do and mend" attitude of our long-gone relatives.

We will embrace their lifestyle again and revel in the abilities we still have, as human beings, to live our lives using our own hands

---

[1] *United Nations Environment Program UNEP*
[2] *The epoch that begins when human activities started to have a significant global impact on Earth's ecosystems (Borenstein, Seth -14 October 2014)*

and minds and bodies—to be explorers again in our world and not passive users of it.

I may have been brought up "old fashioned," but those of us with the skills to grow our own food, treat our own wounds, and build our own houses—in fact, those of us living a more conscious lifestyle—will reap those benefits in a world where the future is a very uncertain one.

HOW NORTH AMERICAN NATIVES AND EARLY PIONEERS MADE PEMMICAN

- By Lex Rooker -

"A starving man will eat with the wolf."

– Oklahoma Native Americans

Pemmican is a concentrated, nutritionally complete food invented by the North American Plains Indians. It was originally made during the summer months from dried lean buffalo meat and rendered fat as a way to preserve and store the meat for use when traveling and as a primary food source during the lean winter months.

When pemmican was discovered by our early frontiersmen (explorers, hunters, trappers, and the like), it became a highly sought-after commodity. The Hudson Bay Company purchased tons of pemmican from the native tribes each year to satisfy the demand.

The basic unit of trade was an animal hide filled with pemmican, sealed with pure rendered fat on the seams, and weighing about

90 pounds. As long as it was kept away from moisture, heat, and direct sunlight, it would last for many years with no refrigeration or other method of preservation.

There appeared to be two types of pemmican. One was a mixture of 50% shredded, dehydrated lean meat and 50% rendered fat by weight. The other mixture was similar but contained 50% rendered fat, 45% shredded dehydrated meat, and 5% dried and ground berries by weight. The berries were typically Saskatoon berries, which grew in abundance in the Great Plains area and are similar to blueberries.

There is much controversy as to whether the natives included the dried berries in the pemmican they made for themselves or whether they added it only to the pemmican they sold to the Hudson Bay Company "because the White Man preferred it that way." I'm of a mind that the natives consumed it both ways.

The journals from the Lewis and Clark expedition clearly state that the Indian tribes they encountered consumed some berries, fruits, and tubers as part of their diet. It seems reasonable that the inclusion of some dried berries would not be out of character for the batches of pemmican made in late summer when ripe berries were available. Berries do not appear to be a nutritional requirement, and they increase the chance of spoilage, so the pemmican formula in this document is for meat and fat only and does not include them.

Please bear in mind that pemmican is NOT a raw food, as the fat needs to be heated above 200°F in order to release it from its cellular structure and drive out the moisture. It is therefore not recommended as part of a daily RAF (Raw Animal Food) diet. However, it is a useful compromise when one is traveling, for use as emergency rations, or when otherwise high-quality raw animal foods are unavailable.

It is important that the lean meat used in pemmican be dehydrated at a temperature below 120°F, and a temperature between 100°F and 115°F is ideal. Temperatures above 120°F will "cook" the meat and will severely compromise the nutritional value of the pemmican.

Federal and State laws require commercial dried meat products like jerky to be raised to a temperature above 150°F, which cooks the meat to a well-done state and makes it totally unsuitable for making pemmican.

Nutritional Qualities

The nutritional qualities of pemmican are unmatched when it is properly made. It can be eaten for months or years as the only food, and no nutritional deficiencies will develop. Yes, that is correct: no fruits, vegetables, grains, or dairy products are required to maintain perfect health—just properly made pemmican and water.

Lack of vitamin C and scurvy are often brought up as a concern. Explorers, hunters, and Native Americans have demonstrated over and over that consuming raw meat or meat that was dried at a temperature below 120°F—as long as there is sufficient fat present to supply enough calories—will maintain perfect health and prevent or cure scurvy. Those that consume salted and preserved meats, biscuits, and other processed foods, even when lemon juice is added to their diet, will often die from scurvy or other nutritional deficiencies.

Calcium and weak bones is another concern. Due to the advertising of the dairy industry, it is believed that milk, cheese, or other dairy products are essential to maintaining good bone density. It has been shown that for people eating a diet of meat and fat, where the animal consumed was allowed to eat its natural diet (usually grass), bones developed normally and remained strong with no sign of deterioration.

For the best quality pemmican, use red meat (deer, beef, elk, bison, etc.) and the rendered fat from these same animals. The animals should be grass fed or have eaten their natural diet in the wild. DO NOT include nuts, seeds, vegetable products, vegetable oils, grains, beans, or dairy products of any kind.

A small amount of well-dried berries (blueberries, Saskatoon, strawberries, etc.) is the only acceptable addition and should not exceed 5% by weight should you choose to include them.

Directions

Ingredients

Use equal amounts, by weight, of very dry red meat and rendered beef tallow. If you have one pound of dried meat, then you will need one pound of rendered beef tallow, two pounds of dried red meat, two pounds of rendered beef tallow, etc.

1. Rendering the Fat

Rendering fat is a simple process, and most of us are familiar with it as it is one of the end results of frying bacon. The process of frying the bacon releases the fat from the cellular structure of the meat and drives off the water. It is the boiling off of the water that actually makes bacon pop and sizzle. The fat itself just turns to a liquid.

Our goal in our rendering process is a bit different from frying bacon in that it is the fat we wish to keep rather than the crisp "cracklin's," which, by the way, taste good when they are still warm with a bit of salt. If you don't want them, they make wonderful dog treats when cool.

We also want to keep the ultimate temperature of the fat as low as possible. I try to keep it below 250°F and usually shoot for a final temperature of around 240°F. You gain nothing by raising the temperature any higher than 240°–250°F other than more damage to the fatty acids, which we want to avoid as much as possible. In short, you need the temperature high enough to boil off the water in a reasonable length of time but as low as practical to maintain the nutritional value and not denature the structure of the fatty acids any more than necessary.

There are two generally accepted methods of rendering. One is to place the fat in a pot and heat it on the stovetop. The other is to place the fat in a roasting pan and put it in the oven with the temperature set between 225°–250°F.

The stovetop method can be completed in about one hour and requires constant attention.

The oven method takes 12 hours or more but can be left unattended during the entire process. I will be covering the stovetop method here with comments on the oven method mixed in but not demonstrated.

Cut the fat into small pieces, about ½" square. Place the diced fat in a stock pot or pan. I select my pot size such that the raw fat fills the pot about ¾ full.

This gives me head room to stir and mix without slinging fat all over the stove or counter. It also fills the pot deep enough with the liquid fat so that I can use a candy thermometer to keep track of the temperature.

If you are using the oven method, just put your fat in a good-sized roasting pan, pop it in the oven set between 225° to 250°F, and then go away for 12 to 24 hours. The oven thermostat will take care of the temperature for you.

Set your burner to medium–high heat, and stir well about every minute or so for the first 10 minutes.

This will keep the bottom from overheating while enough fat is being liberated to cover the bottom of the pan.

After about 10 minutes, you'll see a pool of fat forming on the bottom, which should be merrily boiling away.

You can now rest a bit and stir every 5 minutes or so just to keep things well mixed.

After about 30 minutes, the liquid fat should be deep enough to cover all the chunks, and it should have the appearance of a rolling boil. Reduce the temperature to medium heat, and put a candy thermometer into the fat, making sure it does not touch the bottom of the pan. The water boiling off the fat will keep the temperature around 220°F for a while, but there will come a point when the temperature will start rising.

Keep stirring occasionally, and keep your eye on the thermometer. As it begins to rise, lower the heat setting to keep the temperature around 230° to 240°F. The picture above is after about 45 minutes. The cracklin's are beginning to turn dark in color, the boiling is slowing down, and the temperature of the fat is rising, requiring close attention to the heat setting.

After about one hour, the major boiling action will have stopped, and there will just be small bubbles rising from the fat. Ninety percent of the cracklin's will be a chestnut brown color. The lighter chunks may have a bit more fat left in them, but it is not worth the effort to extract it. If you did the oven method, the fat in your roasting pan should have a similar look.

Now take a good-sized strainer and place it over the container where you will store your rendered fat.

Line the strainer with a single layer of paper towel. This will filter out the sediment and allow just the liquid fat to drip through.

From your pot or roasting pan, pour the fat, cracklin's and all, into the lined strainer. Press on the cracklin's with a serving spoon to press as much fat out of them as possible.

When you've gotten all the fat you can, remove the strainer, and set the container aside to cool. You can sprinkle the cracklin's with a bit of salt and pepper and enjoy them as a snack, set them aside to cool for dog treats, or discard as you wish.

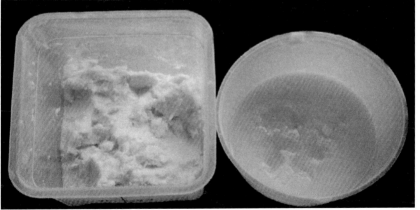

The square tub on the left is tallow that was rendered from the fat of grass-fed animals. It is a deep butter yellow from the carotenoids (the fat soluble vitamin A precursor that gives carrots their orange color) that gets stored in the animal's fat from the green grass they eat. The round bucket on the right is the tallow we just rendered from fat that I got from a local market. The putty color is typical of the fat rendered from grain-fed animals. There is little or no carotene stored in the fat of grain-fed animals.

There is also a major difference in the fatty acid profile of grain-fed versus grass-fed animals. The grass-fed animal fat is between 25 and 50 percent healthy Omega 3 fatty acids. The grain-fed animal's fat is only 2 to 3 percent Omega 3. Omega 3 fatty acids are critical to the development and maintenance of our brain and nerve tissue.

Overall, the meat and fat from grass-fed animals have far greater nutritional value than grain-fed beef. Therefore, if you want to make pemmican that meets all nutritional requirements without the need for additional supplementation, both the lean meat and the fat should come from grass-fed animals.

2. Dried Meat Preparation

To make any useful amount of pemmican, a large quantity of well-dehydrated lean meat is required. You can use a dehydrator or set the oven to the lowest possible temperature (around 150 degrees), and put the strips of meat directly onto the rack. Crack the oven door to prevent moisture buildup. Let the meat dry out for about fifteen hours, or until it is crispy.

Generally, well-dried meat will weigh just slightly less than 1/3 of its raw weight. Therefore, 10 pounds of raw, lean meat will yield about 3 pounds of thoroughly dehydrated meat. Since pemmican is 50% fat and 50% dried meat by weight, 3 pounds of dried meat will make 6 pounds of

pemmican, which will be equal to about 18 pounds of fresh meat.

Start with well-dried red meat: beef, bison, deer, elk, etc. Make sure that the strips of meat are thoroughly dry all the way through. Any observable moisture in the meat will provide an environment for mold and bacteria to grow. If the strips of meat are bent double, they should crack and not be rubbery.

Traditional meat drying - Photo credits: John Johnston

Traditionally, the meat used for pemmican is dried without salt or any other seasoning. If you choose to season your meat, I suggest that you go very lightly—less than half of what you would use for jerky. **Use only dry spices like garlic powder, pepper, cumin, chili powder, salt, etc.**

NEVER, NEVER, NEVER make pemmican with meat that has been marinated in soy sauce, wine, or any marinade that contains sugar of any kind and no vegetable oils of any type.

I always make my pemmican without salt or seasoning and usually prefer eating it that way, but on occasion, I sprinkle a bit of salt or steak seasoning on it at the time I eat it for a change of pace. Be careful—a little bit of seasoning goes a long way in this dense food.

Grind the meat to a fibrous consistency, like a fluffy but slightly chunky mulch. I use a meat grinder with the largest plate (biggest holes) possible. The grinder above is a large #32 manual ChopRite with a 1 ½ horsepower motor in place of the handle and fitted with a "bean" plate that has 3 very large oval holes. If you attempt to use a plate with small holes (½" may work; ¾" or larger is much better), the holes will clog, the grinder could lock up, and you may damage it. Feed one strip at a time, and wait until the exit holes begin to clear before adding the next strip. If it is too chunky and not well shredded, run it through a second time.

Alternatively, you can shred the meat either in a food processor using the steel blade or in a blender. When using these options, it will be helpful to chop the dried meat into smaller pieces, and some people pick up the blender and shake it while grinding to keep the un-ground chunks moving into the blades for a more even grind.

Traditionally, the dry meat was pounded into a powder using rocks. I've tried the pounding method using a hammer and a small

blacksmith's anvil. Unless you have a lot of time and need the exercise, I don't recommend it. It is a lot of work.

Weigh the amount of ground meat that you have, and then weigh out an equal amount of rendered animal fat from the rendering process above. Fat from red meat animals is preferable for the best nutrition and keeping qualities as it becomes very firm when cool, similar to candle wax. No vegetable oils or butter should be used.

Pork or lamb fat can be used but are not recommended as the fatty acid profile is different and they melt at too low a temperature. This can cause the fat and lean to separate in warm weather, so storage becomes a problem unless you are willing to pack the pemmican in liquid-tight containers.

Melt the fat on low heat. It will start to melt at about 120°F.

Try to keep the temperature of the fat below 150°F. You spent time drying the lean meat at low temperatures to maintain its nutritional value, so you don't want to deep fry it when you mix it with the fat.

Mix the shredded meat into the melted fat, and stir until well blended.

The completed mixture should look much like moist, crumbled brownies. The mixture may look "wet," but most of the fat should be absorbed or coating the meat fibers. There should be little or no liquid fat pooling in the bottom of the pan.

Using a sturdy spoon, press the warm mixture into a mold of your choice, or spoon it into a Ziploc plastic bag and press flat, removing as much air as possible. The gray-colored molds below are mini loaf pans that are slightly larger than a cube of butter and hold about 150 grams (1,000 total calories) of pemmican.

The Ziploc bags are sandwich sized and are loaded with about 300 grams (2,000 total calories) of pemmican. When pressed flat, they are about 5" x 6" x ½" thick. Set aside to let cool and harden. The final product will be very hard—almost like a block of wax—and will look a bit like dark oatmeal with some ground raisins stirred in.

If you are using molds such as cupcake tins or loaf pans as above, the pemmican can be removed from the mold once it is hardened and then stored in plastic bags or wrapped in a grease-proof paper.

One convenient method I often use is to press the mixture into lined cupcake pans and then store the resulting hockey pucks with their paper liners in gallon-sized Ziploc plastic bags. Each cupcake in a standard cupcake pan will hold about 75–80 grams (around 500 calories) if you pack them solid to the top.

If you want to keep your pemmican for any length of time, it should be stored in a dark place or wrapped in light-proof paper or aluminum foil as well as placed in a plastic bag to keep out air and moisture.

Pemmican does not require refrigeration and can be kept for years at room temperature as long as it is kept dry and shielded from light and direct heat.

How Much Do I Need?

One half pound of pemmican per day is about the minimum required for a sedentary adult and provides about 1,500 calories. Someone doing light activities might find three-quarters of a pound to be more appropriate to their needs, and this would provide about 2,200 calories. Twice this amount (or more) could easily be necessary when doing hard physical labor (think digging ditches or mountain climbing).

Pemmican is the perfect food for backpacking and hiking. Ten pounds of pemmican will easily sustain a backpacker for a full week, providing one and a half pounds of pemmican per day, which would supply 4,400 calories—enough to support strenuous climbing at high altitudes and in cold weather.

The same 10 pounds of pemmican would supply food for two full weeks of leisure camping activities at three-quarters of a pound per day, providing 2,200 calories.

When made correctly using grass-fed, lean red meat that has been dried at a temperature below 120°F and rendered fat from grass-fed animals, pemmican is a complete food, and no other nutrients or supplements are necessary to completely meet all human nutritional requirements. No other single food is as calorie dense or nutritionally complete.

THE SURVIVAL FOOD OF THE U.S. CIVIL WAR: HOW TO MAKE HARDTACK BISCUITS

- By James Walton -

"An army marches on its stomach."

– Napoleon Bonaparte

Though it may have been fire that brought humans out of the darkness and into the light, just as powerful was the advent of agriculture that allowed us to build communities and stop running and gunning for survival.

Buried in the heap of incredible technologies that catapulted our race to the very moon itself lies an often neglected staple. It was an invention that would have made sea exploration nearly impossible. It was a food that fed soldiers at war for thousands of years. I'm talking about hardtacks.

Not familiar with the name? Well, it goes by many others as well. The fact of the matter is, this staple of the seafaring peoples of old and pioneers alike has been called cabin bread, pilot bread, sea biscuit, sea bread, ship's biscuit, and, as we will discuss now, hardtack.

The journey across the Atlantic was a harsh one that required a food source that could last the long journey. Hardtack offered a carbohydrate energy source that was simply void of moisture. This dried mixture of flour and water was often baked as many as four times to ensure it could be stored for years, if needed, without spoiling.

That said, the hardtacks were not bullet proof. There are stories of sailors opening barrels of hardtack only to find armies of beetles waiting inside and their food storage for the voyage squandered. But these stories were very uncommon. At Wentworth Museum in Pensacola, Florida, you can find a still-edible hardtack from the U.S. Civil War labeled 1862.

In Alaska, people still eat hardtacks and actually enjoy them! Though the hardtack eaten in Alaska today does not come from the recipe we will discuss here, it's still a very simple leavened version with the addition of some fat as well.

Survival kits are required cargo on flights by light aircraft in Alaska, and it seems these hardtacks are a favorite addition to these kits, so much so that they are available everywhere these flights land or take off.

During the Civil War, the South was strangled by a naval blockade that kept fresh wheat out of the hands of the Confederacy. In fact, in the early days of the war, the army was eating hardtacks from the Mexican American War, which had ended in 1848. This astounding fact should drive home the effectiveness of this food.

It was not uncommon for a soldier's full meal to consist of one hardtack for breakfast, one hardtack for lunch, and one for dinner. Now consider the grueling hikes and hand-to-hand combat that ensued. These warriors of our past fought it out with little more than coffee and flour in their stomachs.

Though the Union army had more resources, their soldiers, too, had to depend on hardtacks. Of course, they were not eating biscuits from previous wars, yet these were still rock hard.

To temper its hard nature, they would often dip it into coffee, whiskey, or tea. This acted as a softener. Some of the men would smash them with rifle butts and mix in river water to make a mush. If a frying pan was available, the mush could be cooked into a lumpy pancake. If not, it was dropped directly on campfire coals.

For dessert, hardtack was sometimes crumbled with brown sugar and hot water. If whiskey was available, that was added. The resulting dish was called a pudding.[3]

The best place to find real, honest hardtacks being made is at the popular Civil War reenactments. The men and women who participate in the historic battles often enjoy producing some of the foods of that time. These hardtacks produced by the enactors will be the most authentic you can find outside of making them in your own kitchen.

Hardtacks are also gaining popularity among preppers and survivalists. The tough biscuit is prized for exactly the same reasons

[3] According to historian William Davis

it was in the past. There is an understanding that if it all goes bad, these things will be around. Though they may not be the most delicious option, they could feed you and your family in a bad situation. Thus, hardtacks are becoming part of an extensive inventory of long-term food storage.

The brilliant thing about hard tacks is that they are little more than water, flour, and salt. This is why they last an eternity. The desire to add things for flavor and texture is alluring, but remember, the true purpose of this food is to last forever! The addition of things like fats, which can go rancid, will shorten the lifespan of this food.

I will provide you with a basic recipe for creating these biscuits. What's more important, however, is that you understand the basic ratio. Many people think cooking is about recipes, but really, knowing a ratio is much more powerful than a recipe because it can be manipulated easily. The ratio for hardtacks is 3:1 flour to water. This can be 3 cups of flour to 1 cup of water or 3lbs. to 1lb. or 3 tons to 1 ton. Take this ratio and apply it any way you see fit.

Ingredients

- ❖ 3 cups of flour
- ❖ 1 cup of water
- ❖ 2 teaspoons of salt

Hardware

Cookie sheet or pizza stone ($9 ceramic planter bottom at the local home and garden store)

- ❖ Large mixing bowl
- ❖ Rolling pin
- ❖ Pizza cutter (not necessary)
- ❖ Fork
- ❖ Big nail

Preheat the oven to 350°F.

Add your flour to the large mixing bowl, and stir it around a bit with your fork.

Add the salt to your bowl next, and make sure that it gets well integrated into the mix.

One of the best pieces of advice I can give you when making dough by hand (and if you're making hardtacks, leave the food processor in the cupboard) is to make a well.

Once all of your dry ingredients are incorporated, create a hole in the center of the flour.

Use your fork to push the flour up and around the edges of the bowl.

Pour your water into the well, and slowly begin to incorporate the flour into the water. With your fork, slowly knock the sides into the well, allowing the water to begin to thicken.

This technique with the well allows you to control how much flour you add into your mixture.

Once the mix gets stodgy and doughy, you can turn it out onto a floured table. This mass will still be pretty stick, and it will take some additional flour and elbow grease to make it smooth.

Begin to work the dough by poking at it with your finger tips and folding it over itself. Add flour until it stops sticking to the table and your hands. The dough will get smooth and soft after just a couple minutes.

Once your dough has come together, you can begin to round it out. You want smooth dough that won't stick to your rolling pin or whatever else you use to shape your hardtack. The picture below shows our dough ready for the next steps.

There are several ways you can manipulate your hardtacks into various shapes. I utilize the rolling pin and the pizza cutter. You

could go as crazy as to use a cookie cutter. Just know that although they may be shaped like dinosaurs, these tough biscuits will not soon become a favorite around the house.

One method for forming hardtacks is to use the rolling pin to form a large square. If you have trouble forming the square from your round ball of dough, simply use the pizza cutter to trim the edges. Ensure your hardtacks are at least 1/2 inch thick. Remember these things were actually dinner for the soldiers of the Revolution, Civil War, and maybe even the Roman Legions.

Use a common household nail to poke holes into the hard tack. This allows the center of your biscuit to dry out quicker and more thoroughly in the oven. For a  nice-sized square hardtack, poke 16 holes straight through the dough.

Another method for shaping your hardtacks is to break your dough down into smaller portions. These portions will cook quicker and can be more easily divided among others should the need arise.

From here, shape the portions into smaller circles. These will become your individual portions. Though smaller than the large, square method featured above, these will also need holes punched in them using the nail.

When you think about this ancient recipe and how it must have been prepared all those years ago, it's really hard to throw these things on a Teflon-coated cookie sheet and bake them like chocolate chip cookies. Invest in a clay planter bottom at your local home and garden store.

These are an incredible tool for baking breads or making stellar pizza out of a home oven. They cost about $9 and last a long time. The clay is highly effective because it holds heat so well.

Lay your hardtacks out, and give them enough space to bake evenly. Place them in the oven for 30 minutes.

This 30-minute cook time is merely the first of at least two bakes these hard biscuits will go through. This process, although time consuming, will ensure that there is no remaining moisture in your hardtacks. Any moisture becomes the complete enemy of this process of shelf stability. Some old recipes call for three and even four times in the oven. These biscuits must have been closer kin to bricks than food.

Once your first 30 minutes is over, pull out the hardtacks and allow them to cool. The steam will come out of them, and they will get pretty hard, although they will not be hard or dry enough to store at this point. After having cooled them for about 20 minutes, place them back in the oven. This time set your timer for one hour.

It will be this bake that thoroughly dries your biscuits and also begins to give them a pleasing bit of color.

Following the last hour of baking, turn your oven off. DO NOT REMOVE THE HARDTACKS. Instead, leave your pilot's biscuits in the turned-off oven. Let the heat slowly drop in the oven while your biscuits slowly dry even further. This is a great practice for really zapping any remaining moisture left inside.

At this point, you have created some decent shelf-stable hardtacks. Now, unlike most foods you spend time making from scratch, I can't say you will be delighted to try them. They are dry and hard. Those are basically the two features for your palate when it comes to hardtacks.

It won't get much better than that, and really, it shouldn't. Remember, if you decide to flavor them up with butter or herbs, this will simply add ingredients that will drastically shorten the shelf life of your hardtacks. Keep it simple, and they will last forever.

Also, when you read about just how hard these HARDtacks are, you must understand that there aren't words that do them justice. If you do decide to taste the fruits of your labor, I advise you to take some precautions. Make sure you are chewing with the best teeth you have. If there is anything loose or filled in there, it may very well come out or even shatter.

All jesting aside, this is an ancient food that has carried entire nations through tough times. If you follow the recipe above and store your hardtacks properly, there is no doubt these biscuits will do the same for you and your family if that day ever comes.

HOW TO RENDER LARD

- By Dana Rem -

"Let food be thy medicine [...]."

– Hippocrates

In the 19th century, lard was used in American households similarly to butter. It was a cooking and baking staple.

In 1854, J. Stonesifer of Boonesborogh patented a lamp that specifically used lard as fuel. A screw-driven piston forced lard up into the chamber around the wick, where it burned to form an efficient source of portable light. A tin loop handle with a hole in it was used for hanging.

Lard's popularity decreased during the Industrial Revolution as vegetable oil become more affordable and common.

In the 20th century it was used as a substitute for butter during World War II. By the end of the century, it was considered to be less healthy than vegetable oil, but recent studies suggest otherwise.

Rendered lard can be used to make soap, but it can also be used as a biofuel. It was also applied as a poultice to burns, cuts, and inflamed areas. It can be used as a balm, and it moisturizes and protects the skin from chapping and cracking. You can also mix it with beeswax and use it to refurbish and maintain wood and leather.

The best use for lard is actually meat preservation. Meat will last up to a year if it's conserved in lard.

How to Render Lard

The first step is preparing the fat. I used the back fat, but leaf fat can also be used. This fat was fresh, so I left it to cure with salt for two days. This is not mandatory, but it gives it a better taste and helps to conserve it. Afterwards it should be put in the smoker for one day to dry and then left to smoke for two days with cold smoke. Again, this is done for the same reason as the curing: taste and longer preservation.

Chop the fat into small pieces as equally as you can, about ½" square.

Put them in a pot on medium heat.

Stir every minute or so for the first ten minutes with a wooden spoon and afterwards every five minutes. It's good to add a little bit of water too so that the fat won't stick to the pan. When it really starts boiling, reduce the heat.

When the lardons turn golden, remove the pot from the heat and wait for five more minutes before clearing away the lardons. They will continue to cook during that time.

If you remove the pot as soon as they are done, the lard will burn and won't be white. It would still taste great however, and you can still use it. I used around four and a half pounds of fat, and I kept it on the heat for about 35–40 minutes.

Remove the delicious, crispy lardons with a slotted spoon or with a strainer.

Next filter the lard through a fine-meshed sieve. Place the lard in glass jars or enamel metal containers or pots.

To prevent the jars from breaking, you can either heat them up a little bit before pouring the lard or wait a couple of minutes for the lard to get a little bit cooler.

Don't wait too long, however, as it will turn solid, but you can always heat it up again. The metal containers have to be enamel or the lard will go rancid.

Screw the cap of the jar on tightly after the lard is solid.

The lard will last up to a year, or up to two years if the fat is smoked beforehand. The containers have to be placed in a cool, dry, dark place.

Preserving Meat for a Year with Lard

If you want to preserve meat, cut it into pieces and put it into jars. Then pour hot lard over it, making sure you cover the meat and have at least about an inch of clear lard. Wait for the lard to solidify, and then screw on the caps.

You can use it to conserve raw meat, but it will last only about a month. If you want to conserve it up to a year, you have to smoke the meat beforehand for a couple of days.

Then you can fry it and place it in the containers, covering it with lard. You can also do the same with homemade sausages.

The best way to cook this meat is just to put it in a pan with a spoonful of lard until it's hot. The pieces of meat will be very tender and juicy.

Be very careful with this preservation method as the meat usually doesn't last more than a couple of months. The jars or metal containers have to be stored in a cool, dry place.

HOW TO MAKE CHONOS, THE INCA SURVIVAL FOOD

- By Julie Danes -

"If you don't prepare, you could lose everything. If you prepare for the worst and nothing happens, you've lost nothing."

— Gerald Celente

South America and potatoes are most likely not the first things to come to mind when talking about survival food. But it may surprise you to learn that they are an important part of the subject. This is due to the ingenuity of Peru's Inca civilization and the versatility of the lowly spud. To this day, potatoes are transformed into a long-lasting, versatile food called chuños. This is done using a method that is the forefather of our modern freeze-drying.

Most people don't realize that some of the food they eat is preserved using centuries-old processes. These methods of keeping food didn't originate in a sterile laboratory. The ideas were born years ago in rocky fields on high mountainsides in freezing temperatures. The ancients worried they would not have enough to eat if their crops failed or if hunting was scarce. These people were the original food preservation experts or survivalists with their descendants still practicing many of their old ways.

Why the Incas Preserved Foods

Famine or food shortages were a major concern in the life of the Incas. One bad crop year could mean starvation. This, along with the reasons below, encouraged them to find ways to store food and prolong its usefulness.

- ❖ Natural disasters such as drought, hailstorms, tornadoes, fire and floods could destroy fields in minutes. Crops were also lost to animals, insects and some plant diseases.

- ❖ War diminished food stockpiles and it was common for enemies to set fire to fields.

- ❖ Preserved foodstuffs were a commodity that could be easily stored, transported and traded.

- ❖ Many times, stored food was more valuable than gold or gems.

Archaeologists have unearthed evidence of even prehistoric man preserving the food they gathered or hunted. There have been examples of food that is thousands of years old found in various places across the globe. Not necessarily edible according to our modern standards, but definitely well-preserved.

Methods Used by the Inca Civilization

Incas in the highest reaches of Peru were using the freeze-wet-dry-repeat cycle for creating chuños as early as 3000 BC. Along with potatoes, other tubers, root vegetables and starchy foods received the same treatment. Each of these foods could be easily reconstituted with water to create nourishing meals. When properly stored away from moisture, the chuños or other similarly preserved foods could last for decades.

The Inca Indians were ahead of their time when it came to both farming and food preservation. Along with the freeze-drying technique for chuños, they understood the concept of freezing foods. The use of the sun and air for drying meats, fish and other edibles was also practiced. Salt was abundant near the coastlines and was used for curing as well as seasoning.

Runners from the various cultures served as both messengers and early day deliverymen. Methods of improved food production and preservation could be shared between the far-flung tribes. Increased productivity and improved ability to survive times of famine were due in part to the sharing of knowledge.

The word chuño is an Andean term that means "wrinkle." *El chuño*, as it is called, is the result of preserving the potato through dehydration. We assume that the name is due to the look that the potatoes take on during the process, which we will explain to you step by step:

Selection of potatoes

It is important that they are as similar as possible in size and

shape. For this article, we have selected potatoes whose total weight is 750 grams.

Freeze first

In the past, the Quechua and Aymara tribes made chuño by placing the potatoes outside to freeze during the snowfall. Currently we have refrigerators, so freezing them is a lot easier for us today.

As seen in the picture, we must place the potatoes to be frozen in a freezer for 24 hours.

Place in the sun

At this time, you need to place them in the sun when it's at its most intense. Ten to seventeen hours is recommended; then express.

You will notice that the potatoes adopt a wrinkled appearance (remember that is precisely what the term chuño means) and a soft texture. At this point in the process, you must squeeze to extract as much water as possible from the potatoes. In addition to wrinkling, they are significantly reduced in size.

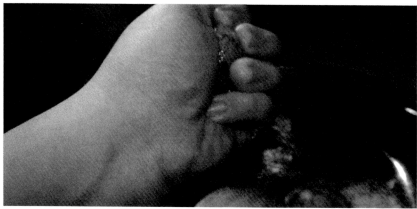

Refreeze

Once you have dried them in the sun, you should put them back in the refrigerator for the same amount of time as the first time.

Repeat in the sun

This time you will do it at the same time and during the same time period, but unlike the previous time, you will notice how the shell of the potatoes  begins to become easy to detach.   As seen in the picture, the potatoes continue to reduce their size, and where the shell has already detached, it begins to darken.

Let harden

When you have frozen and sunbathed the potatoes twice, you must peel them completely and squeeze them to the maximum.

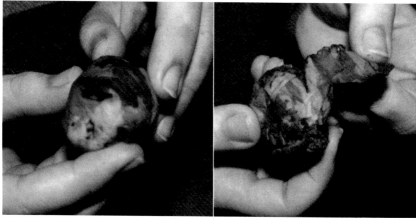

You will notice that as they finish drying, they become very hard and dark. At this time, the potatoes will have already lost two-thirds of their size; this is because they have already lost all the water that they contained.

As you can see in the picture, even though the potatoes selected for this article went from weighing 750 grams to now weighing only 250, since all were selected uniformly, they still retain similar sizes between them.

This method is used to preserve food in a prolonged way, so potatoes that go through this process until becoming chuño can be stored almost anywhere as long as it is a dry place that is away from humidity. The estimated time of preservation is indefinite. Some say that these potatoes can last several years, but it is recommended not to exceed 12 months. This and other techniques of preservation of food are proof of the ingenuity of the human race in favor of their survival. It is important to learn a little about these kinds of things, not only because they are useful but also because it is worth knowing about the inventions of our ancestors.

LOST PIONEER RECIPES FROM THE 18TH CENTURY

- By James Walton -

"You don't need a silver fork to eat good food."

– Paul Prudhomme

Whether pushing west into the dangerous and unknown territories or roughing it through times of economic depression, Americans have often used very minimal ingredients to make meals.

In these times of extreme need, Americans brought knowledge from their home country or used whatever ingredients were cheap and plentiful to create meals to sustain them.

From these desperate times, some classic recipes emerged.

Bacon Fried Apples

- ❖ 5 slices of bacon
- ❖ 6 Granny Smith apples
- ❖ Fresh butter

Fry your bacon in a Dutch oven. Set it aside. Peel and slice your apples into similar sizes. Put the apples in the Dutch oven, and fry in the bacon grease until softened. Remove them and cover with crumbled bacon. Top with some fresh butter.

Bean Sausage

- ❖ 1 cup soaked lentils, dried peas, lima beans, or beans
- ❖ 1 egg
- ❖ 1/2 cup dried breadcrumbs
- ❖ 1/2 tsp salt
- ❖ 1 tsp sage
- ❖ 1/4 cup fat

Prep Time: 20 minutes; Cook Time: 10 minutes

Mash together the cooked beans in a large bowl. Add the rest of the ingredients, and mix well. Form portions of this mix into sausage shapes. Coat with flour, and fry until crispy on all sides.

Vinegar Lemonade

Mix 2 tablespoons of apple cider vinegar into a 12-ounce glass of water. Stir in 2 tablespoons of sugar to taste.

The pioneers used vinegar for numerous reasons. One reason was to add vitamin C to their diets.

Poor Man's Meal

- ❖ 3 potatoes

- ❖ 1 onion
- ❖ 4 hot dogs
- ❖ 4 Tbsp tomato sauce

Prep Time: 5 minutes; Cook Time: 10 minutes

Peel and dice your potatoes to a similar size as your onions. Cook them over medium heat until the onions begin to go translucent. Slice your hot dogs, and add them to the mix. Finally, add your sauce, and simmer until the potatoes are soft.

Hot Water Cornbread

- ❖ 4 cups of boiling water
- ❖ 1 cup yellow cornmeal
- ❖ 1/4 cup flour
- ❖ 1/2 cup canola oil
- ❖ 1 tsp salt
- ❖ 1 Tbsp sugar (optional)

Prep Time: 5 minutes; Cook Time: 10 minutes

Combine the dry ingredients in a bowl. Add boiling water, and stir until you get the consistency of pancake batter. Use a wooden spoon to do the stirring.

Heat about a 1/4 inch of oil in a cast iron skillet on medium-high heat. Use about a quarter cup of batter per cake. Pour the batter into your hot oil, and fry the cake on both sides. Delicious with fresh honey.

Buttery Sweet Potatoes

- ❖ 6 sweet potatoes
- ❖ 1 Tbsp butter
- ❖ 1/2 cup milk
- ❖ 1/2 cup cream
- ❖ Salt and pepper
- ❖ A dash of nutmeg

Prep Time: 10 minutes; Cook Time: 15 minutes

Start by peeling and dicing your sweet potatoes. Be sure to cut them all into similar sizes so they cook evenly. Place them in a pot with your milk and cream. Simmer the potatoes for about 10 minutes or until they are softened enough that a fork will pierce them without resistance. Mash them with the back of a wooden spoon then add your butter and seasonings.

Scrambled Dinner

- ❖ 3 large eggs
- ❖ 3 tablespoons butter
- ❖ 3 slices of white bread ripped into bite-sized pieces
- ❖ 1 can asparagus

Prep Time: 5 minutes; Cook Time: 5 minutes

Set your stovetop to medium heat. Melt the butter in a large cast iron skillet, and allow it to begin to foam a bit. Add your ripped-up bread to the butter, and make sure the bread gets coated thoroughly.

Allow it a couple minutes of continuous movement to toast a bit.

Crack your eggs in a bowl, and add about a tablespoon of water. Whip the eggs until fluffy, and add to your toasted bread in the skillet. I prefer to push the bread to one side and begin to scramble the eggs on the empty side. Once the eggs are firmed up, add your can of asparagus shoots. Season with salt and pepper.

1875 Cottage Cheese

Allow milk to form clabber. Skim off cream once clabbered. Set the clabbered milk on very low heat, and cut in 1 inch squares. Place a colander into the clabber. Skim off whey that rises into the colander.

When the clabber becomes firm, rinse with cold water. Squeeze liquid out, and press into a ball. Crumble into a bowl. Mix curds with thick cream.

Blue-Flower Featherbed

- ❖ 1 loaf of crusty bread
- ❖ 1 1/4 cups of Muenster cheese
- ❖ 1 3/4 cups of Ricotta cheese
- ❖ 1 cup of green onions
- ❖ 6 eggs
- ❖ 1 cup of milk

Prep Time: 5 minutes; Cook Time: 50 minutes

Butter a 9-inch cast iron skillet. Slice your loaf into 12 slices about 1/2 inch thick. Layer your bread, cheeses, and green onions until you have used up all the bread. Whisk your eggs and milk together with some salt and pepper. Pour the mixture over the layers. Cover this, and allow it to sit in the refrigerator for at least an hour. Preheat the oven to 350 degrees. Bake for 50 minutes or until the egg mix begins to puff and brown.

Side Pork and Mormon Gravy

- ❖ 8 thick slices side pork (or thick-cut bacon strips)
- ❖ 4 tablespoons meat drippings
- ❖ 3 tablespoons flour
- ❖ 2 cups milk
- ❖ Salt, pepper, and paprika

Cook Time: 5 minutes

Begin by frying your bacon on both sides in a cast iron skillet till crisp. Add the meat drippings to the pan, and remove the bacon. Take the pan off the heat, and add your flour. Stir this in until the fat and flour mix gets nice and smooth. This mixture is called a roux and will be used to thicken your gravy.

Put the pan back over the heat to allow the roux to cook for about a minute. Remove the pan again, and slowly add the milk, about a half cup at a time. Allow the milk to thicken, and stir it smooth before adding the next batch. The gravy will continue to thicken until your mix comes to a simmer.

Cooked Cabbage Salad

- ❖ 1 pint or more of chopped cooked cabbage
- ❖ 1 egg well beaten

- ❖ 1/4 cup vinegar
- ❖ 1 tsp butter
- ❖ Dash of salt and pepper

Prep Time: 5 minutes; Cook Time: 5 minutes;

Using honey or sugar, sweeten the salad to your taste. Simmer a few minutes, and add 1/2 cup of thick, fresh cream. Serve immediately.

Lemon Pie Filling

- ❖ 1 cup of hot water
- ❖ 1 Tbsp cornstarch
- ❖ 1 cup white sugar
- ❖ 1 Tbsp butter
- ❖ Juice and grated rind of one lemon
- ❖ 1 egg

Prep Time: 10 minutes; Cook Time: 5 minutes

Add everything but the egg to a saucepan, and bring to a simmer for a few minutes. Take a ladleful of the mix and mix it with your egg in a separate bowl. This will keep your egg from scrambling. Add this mix back to the remainder of the filling. Simmer until it thickens. This can be used in pies, turnovers, etc.

Potato Pancakes

- ❖ 1/2 cup milk
- ❖ 2 cups flour

- ❖ 1 egg
- ❖ 2 cups mashed potatoes
- ❖ 1 tsp salt
- ❖ 5 tsp baking powder

Prep Time: 10 minutes

Mix the potato, flour, salt, and baking soda in a bowl before adding in the remaining ingredients. Form the cakes in your hands, and fry in a cast iron skillet over medium–high heat. Eat these with butter, sour cream, or even hot sauce.

Bean Soup

- ❖ 1 quart water
- ❖ 1 cup beans
- ❖ 1 Tbsp onion juice
- ❖ 2 tsp salt
- ❖ 1–2 large onions, sliced or chunked
- ❖ 1/4 tsp mustard
- ❖ 2 Tbsp flour mixed with 2 Tbsp cold water
- ❖ 1 ham hock

Cook Time: 45 minutes

Soak your beans the night before as this will help soften them and will greatly reduce cooking time. Add everything to a pot, and simmer for 45 minutes. If your water begins to evaporate, simply add more.

Pepper and Eggs

- ❖ 3 large peppers
- ❖ 1 Tbsp vegetable oil or lard
- ❖ 4 eggs

Prep Time: 5 minutes; Cook Time: 5 minutes

Cut your peppers in half lengthwise before removing the seeds. Slice the peppers, and fry them in a medium skillet in the oil or lard. Whip up the 4 eggs, and add them to the peppers. Season with salt and pepper.

Dumplings

- ❖ 2 cups flour
- ❖ 4 tsp baking powder
- ❖ 2 Tbsp chilled fat drippings
- ❖ 1 tsp salt
- ❖ 1 cup milk, meat stock, or water

Prep Time: 15 minutes; Cook Time: 30 minutes

Sift salt together with all of your dry ingredients then cut with fat. This will make your dough turn crumbly, and that's what you want. Slowly add milk or water to create a soft dough. Roll out and put on the pre-greased pan. These could be used in soups or stews and should be cooked for thirty minutes.

Beans & Ham Hocks

- ❖ 4 or 5 smoked ham hocks
- ❖ 1 lb. dry pinto beans
- ❖ 1 chopped yellow onion
- ❖ Bay leaf
- ❖ 2 1/2 tsp black pepper
- ❖ Salt to taste

Cook Time: 1 hour

Boil your beans in a large pot with the onion, bay leaf, and ham hocks. Cook this pot over a comfortable simmer until the beans are soft. Finally, add your seasonings and simmer for another 15 minutes.

Milk Toast

- ❖ 1 pint scalded milk
- ❖ 1/2 tsp salt
- ❖ 2 Tbsp of butter
- ❖ 4 Tbsp cold water
- ❖ 2 1/2 Tbsp bread flour
- ❖ 6 slices dry toast

Prep Time: 5 minutes; Cook Time: 5 minutes

Add your water and flour to a skillet, and begin to heat on medium. Stir constantly until you have a nice creamy paste. Add the milk slowly, and allow it to thicken as well. Cover and cook on low for about 15 minutes. Sprinkle with salt, and add the butter in small pieces. Dip your toast slices on one side into the sauce. Once softened, remove, and pour the remaining sauce on the toast.

Cinnamon Sugar Toast

- ❖ 1 loaf crusty bread
- ❖ 1 stick butter
- ❖ 1 cup sugar
- ❖ 2 Tbsp. cinnamon

Prep Time: 1 minute; Cook Time: 3 minutes

Mix your sugar and cinnamon together. Cut your loaf into 1/2-inch slices, and grill, broil, or toast them. Spread your butter on the toast while it's still hot. Sprinkle your cinnamon sugar mix on top, and serve.

Cornmeal Mush

- ❖ 1 cup cornmeal
- ❖ 2 cups bone broth
- ❖ Bacon grease

Prep Time: 8 hours; Cook Time: 5 minutes

Combine the cornmeal and the bone broth. Mix thoroughly, and place in a loaf pan. Allow the mix to sit overnight in the cooler. Slice thick rounds, and fry in bacon grease. Fry each side to a crisp golden brown.

Elk Backstrap with Spiced Plum Sauce

Sauce:

- ❖ 1/2 cup minced onion
- ❖ 1/2 cup cider vinegar
- ❖ 1 pound ripe plums, pitted and quartered
- ❖ 2 Tbsp sugar
- ❖ 1 cinnamon stick
- ❖ Salt and pepper
- ❖ 8 elk or venison backstraps cut into 4–5 oz. medallions

Prep Time: 20 minutes; Cook Time: 1 hour

Combine your onion and vinegar in a non-reactive saucepan, and cook over low heat until the onion has softened. Add everything else for the sauce to the pot, and cook over medium–low heat until thick and reduced to a jam consistency. This could take up to an hour.

Meat:

Cook the elk medallions for about 3 minutes on each side, and allow to rest for 5 minutes before serving.

Corned Beef

- ❖ 10 pounds of beef brisket
- ❖ 2 cups salt
- ❖ 2 cups molasses
- ❖ 2 Tbsp saltpeter

- ❖ 1 Tbsp ground pepper
- ❖ 1 Tbsp cloves
- ❖ Bourbon or whiskey

Prep Time: 10 days

Rinse the beef well before coating the remaining ingredients. Add the bourbon or whiskey at the end to rub the meat down. This will keep mold growth down and help the meat's flavor as well. Turn every 24 hours, and add more salt when the amount used has dissolved.

After 10 days, rinse well and use in soups or stews or slow cook on the grill. Drink the rest of the bourbon while you wait during the 10 days.

Soda Biscuits

- ❖ 3 1/3 cups flour
- ❖ 1 tsp baking soda
- ❖ 1 tsp salt
- ❖ 1/4 cup milk

Prep Time: 15 minutes; Cook Time: 20 minutes

Preheat the oven to 400°F. Mix together your dry ingredients. Add the milk, and work the mixture with your hands until you have a nice dough that can be rolled out. Punch out circles using a cup or cutter. Bake in the oven for 15–20 minutes.

Skillet Trout

- ❖ 3 trout, dressed (head, fins, tail, and guts removed)
- ❖ 1/4 cup cornmeal
- ❖ 1/4 cup flour
- ❖ 1 tsp salt

Prep Time: 5 minutes; Cook Time: 5 minutes

Mix together your dry ingredients. Pat dry your trout fillets before dredging them in your mixture of dry ingredients. Once they are well coated, immediately fry them in hot oil in a cast iron skillet until crispy and golden brown.

Winter Red Flannel Hash

- ❖ 1 1/2 cups chopped corned beef
- ❖ 1 1/2 cups chopped cooked beets
- ❖ 1 medium onion, chopped
- ❖ 4 cups chopped cooked potatoes

Prep Time: 10 minutes; Cook Time: 5 minutes

In a large bowl, mix together your chopped ingredients. Heat some oil in a cast iron skillet on high. Add your mix of chopped items to the hot oil, and drop the heat down to low. Allow 10 full minutes on low without disturbing the mix. This will form a good crust. Turn out onto a plate, and serve with eggs.

Mormon Johnnycake

- ❖ 2 cups yellow cornmeal
- ❖ 1/2 cup flour
- ❖ 1 tsp baking soda
- ❖ 1 tsp salt
- ❖ 2 cups buttermilk

Prep Time: 5 minutes; Cook Time: 20 minutes

Preheat the oven to 425°F. Combine your dry ingredients first before adding the wet, and mix the whole batter thoroughly. Dump the mix into a buttered cast iron skillet, and bake for 20 minutes.

Spotted Pup

- ❖ 1 lb. cooked rice
- ❖ 2 cups milk
- ❖ 2 eggs
- ❖ 1 Tbsp cinnamon
- ❖ 1/4 cup sugar
- ❖ A handful of raisins

Prep Time: 10 minutes; Cook Time: 15 minutes

Whip together the eggs and milk before combining all ingredients in a Dutch oven to cook until the mixture becomes creamy and sweetened. This should take no longer than 15 minutes over a medium–low heat.

Oatmeal Pancakes

- ❖ 2 cups oatmeal
- ❖ 1 Tbsp melted fat
- ❖ 1/8 tsp salt
- ❖ 1 egg beaten in 1 cup of milk
- ❖ 1 cup sifted flour
- ❖ 1 tsp baking powder

Prep Time: 5 minutes; Cook Time: 2 minutes per cake

Add the oatmeal, flour, and baking powder to a bowl. Mix well. Combine with the remaining ingredients. Fry this batter in a cast iron skillet over high heat. Serve with honey or syrup.

Spider Cornbread

- ❖ 2 cups sour milk
- ❖ 1 1/2 cups cornmeal
- ❖ 1 tsp soda
- ❖ 2 eggs
- ❖ 2 Tbsp butter
- ❖ 1 tsp salt

Prep Time: 5 minutes; Cook Time: 20 minutes

Preheat the oven to 350°F. The use of sour milk is what makes this dish interesting. Mix your dry ingredients together first before stirring in your wet ingredients. Add the batter to a hot, buttered cast iron skillet. Cook in the oven for 20 minutes.

Mud Apples

- ❖ 4 large apples
- ❖ A bucket of mud

Prep Time: 15 minutes; Cook Time: 45 minutes

For this recipe, you should really have a campfire.

Using the mud, coat your apples completely in a nice layer. Spread the coals of your fire, and lay the mud-coated apples on them. Build up the sides with the smoldering coals. Allow the apples to bake and the "clay" to harden around them for 45 minutes.

Be careful once they are done as you will have to remove the hardened clay shell and they will be smoking hot inside as well. Spoon the cooked apple out and enjoy!

Gorge Pasta

- ❖ 1 cup raw macaroni
- ❖ 1 can stewed tomatoes
- ❖ 1 lb. cheddar cheese

Cook Time: 15 minutes

Cook your pasta until it is nice and tender. Drain and allow it to steam for a minute or two. Add the stewed tomatoes, cheddar cheese, and hot macaroni to a bowl, and stir around until the cheese is completely melted.

Glazed Turnips

- ❖ 5 whole turnips
- ❖ 2 Tbsp butter
- ❖ 1 Tbsp salt
- ❖ 1 Tbsp sugar

Prep Time: 5 minutes; Cook Time: 10 minutes

Dice the turnips into nice, healthy-sized pieces. I would look for at least a half-inch in size on the dice. After dicing all of your turnips, melt your butter in a skillet, and toss the turnips in. Coat them well with the butter, and allow to cook for about five minutes. Next sprinkle the turnips with salt and sugar, and allow to cook for another five minutes. By this point, they should be softened and ready to eat.

HOW THE PIONEERS BUILT THEIR SMOKEHOUSES

- By John Paicu -

"Smoke me a kipper, I'll be back for breakfast"

– Ace Rimmer, Red Dwarf

Once upon a time, every house had a smokehouse. Households would make their own smokehouses from hardwood and brick, and then they would use it to prepare all kinds of meats. Preserved in cool, dry places, the smoked products would last up to one year. Even though very few people nowadays still use traditional smokehouses, those that care about eating healthy, delicious meat should know that building a smokehouse in your own backyard is easier than it may look.

Smoking is one of the best, tastiest, and healthiest way to prepare meat, fish, and even cheese, and the pioneers have been doing it for centuries. But back then they didn't do it to improve the taste of the meat. The main purpose of a smokehouse was to preserve the meat. Preservation was done by sustained smoking (often for more than two weeks using cold smoke) and salt curing. The pioneers would leave the products in the smoker for extended periods of time (sometimes up to two years) because they didn't have any refrigeration systems.

Because we live in the world of the processed food industry—where nothing we buy from supermarkets is healthy anymore—it's only natural to want to reassess our options and find a better way to cook our meat. Smoking is one of those methods that helps you prepare meat the natural way, with no preservatives. It lasts longer, and it tastes delicious. To get started, all you need to do is build the smokehouse, buy the meat, light the fire, and allow the smoke to work its magic.

There are different types of smokehouses that you can build, although the easiest and safest model is made of hardwood. Commonly referred to as a "slow cooking oven," the temperature in a smokehouse shouldn't exceed 200 degrees Fahrenheit.

Step-by-step Guide on How to Build a Smokehouse The Pioneer Way

First, you have to define the area where you want to build the smokehouse [Figure 1]. After the area has been properly outlined, the next step is to dig the groove. The conventional shape looks almost like a square-shaped dumbbell. The fire pit must be built downhill to allow the smoke to go upward.

The square-shaped hole for the fire pit has a diameter of 16'' in length, 20'' in width, and 8'' in depth. The depth of the smokehouse varies since it has to be built upward to allow the smoke to circulate properly. Next, you have to dig a tunnel from the fire pit all the way to the foundation of your smokehouse. The tunnel should be 7.5 feet in length.

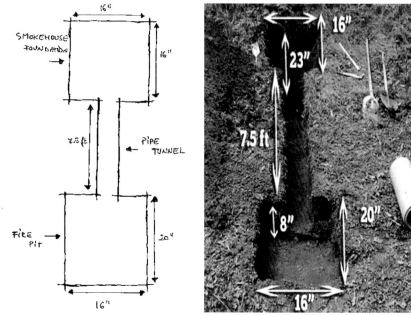

Figure 1.

As for the foundation of the smokehouse, the diameter should be 16'' in length, 16'' in width, and 23'' in depth. Between the fire pit and the foundation, a delivery pipe is placed to help direct the smoke to the meat.

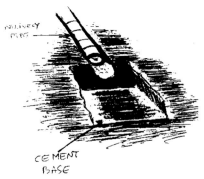

Figure 2.

The fire pit is made up of firebricks, and you can use concrete for the foundation [Figure 3]. Use the same concrete to isolate the delivery pipe, and in the front of the fire box, install an iron door so that you can place the wood that needs to burn to generate the smoke.

Figure 3.

The pipe installed to connect the fire box to the smokehouse should have an upward pitch. It will curve to reach the smokehouse right in the middle of the cement floor [Figure 4].

Figure 4.

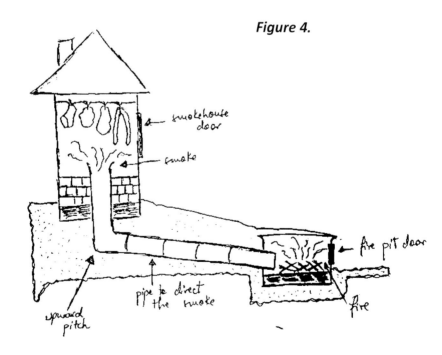

Building The SmokeHouse

Now that the firebox and has been completed and the delivery pipe has been properly installed and fitted, it's time to move on to building the smokehouse.

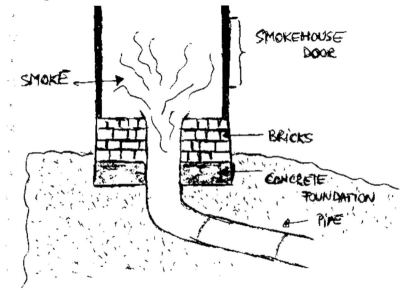

Figure 5.

Pour a concrete foundation, and let it dry [Figure 5]. If the depth of the foundation is 23″, the foundation should be about 17″. Move on to building the walls of the smokehouse from bricks.

About five layers of bricks should be enough (This means that your foundation will be about 10″ in height.).

For the wooden foundation of the smokehouse, the best type of hardwood is cherry, apple, pear, or apricot. You can use pallets because they're durable and conveniently priced. The base of your smokehouse should be square-shaped and should mold perfectly after the brick foundation. Since this is a small-sized smokehouse, try not to exceed 3 feet in height.

Considering the brick foundation is 16″ x 16″, the base of the wooden smokehouse should also be 16″ x 16″. In height, 3 feet for the walls and 1 foot for the roof should be enough [Figure 6].

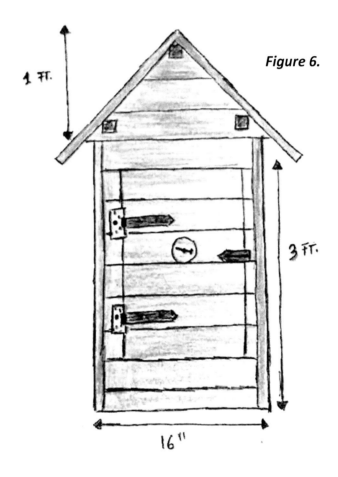

Figure 6.

Figure 7.

Stick to a conventional triangular shape for the roof, and at the end, drill a hole on one of the sides for the chimney. Don't drill the roof onto the walls of the smokehouse. It should be detachable so that you can check the meat whenever you want and even remove the product with ease if you don't want to use the door.

Inside the smokehouse, you should place wooden racks. (Don't forget to sculpt several V-notches at a distance of 0.5 inches from one another.) This will help you place the steel hooks you will use to hang the meat on.

After the smokehouse has been completed [Figure 8] and installed on top of the brick foundation, cover the pipe with dirt, and place wooden pallets on top [Figure 9]. You will use these as steps to get to the smokehouse and get the smoked products.

Paint the smokehouse whatever color you like (although it's recommended to be dark brown), and have a thermostat installed in the middle of the door to help you monitor the temperature inside.

Figure 8.

Figure 9.

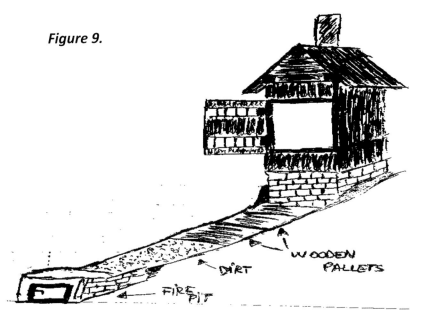

How to Smoke Meat The Right Way

Curing (or smoking) meat in smokers is no longer a necessity. The pioneers did it because they didn't have refrigerators, freezers, or any additional storage facilities to place their products in and extend shelf life. The process, however, is still one of the most delicious and healthiest way to consume and prepare meat, fish, and even cheese. Basically, curing means "flavoring" meat products (pork, beef, chicken, turkey, duck, etc.) with smoke.

Curing differs from barbecuing and grilling. Smoked meat is prepared at temperatures between 52°F and 140°F, and the process can last from several hours to two weeks. Cured meat is thoroughly cooked inside and out. You may choose to smoke your meat for just an hour or two to give is a nice smoked color on the

97

outside and keep it moist on the inside and then cook it once again in the oven or in the frying pan before consuming it.

Some key benefits of smoking:

- ❖ Extended shelf life
- ❖ Kills certain types of bacteria
- ❖ Prevents mold accumulation
- ❖ Prevents fats from getting that rancid, sour taste
- ❖ Improves flavor and taste
- ❖ Changes the color of the meat—smoked meat just looks delicious!

The longer you keep the products in the smokehouse, the saltier they'll be. This happens because when cured, the meat loses moisture. Heavily cured meat products have an extended shelf life and can be consumed for months on end.

HOW THE EARLY PIONEERS BUILT THE SELF-FEEDING FIRE

- By James Walton -

*"Some Native people suggest that
one should test how cold the hands are by
touching the thumb to the little finger of the
same hand. As soon as you cannot carry
out this exercise you are reaching a
dangerous state of incapacity, and you
should immediately take steps to warm up."*

— M. Kochanski

Spanning some 300 years from the first contact of settlers in Jamestown, pioneers have explored their way across this massive continent. The pioneers pushed westward and touched every part of this great land. Farmers, fur traders, miners, and surveyors all played a crucial role in expanding the nation.

All that said, these men were not staying at the Holiday Inn during their explorations. Pioneers were surviving out in the elements. Whether summer or winter, these brave men and women forged on against the worst the North American climate could throw at them. On this nasty road, self-reliance was everything.

It took a great deal of ingenuity to battle the elements, the wildlife, the germs, and the native peoples as these pioneers traveled on their way. Things like sewing, weaving, canning, and gunsmithing were skills that simply had to be learned when you were surrounded by thousands of miles of hostile wilderness. Of course, they paid special attention to the survival basics, and water, fire, and shelter were prioritized above all else.

The self-feeding fire was the pioneers' answer to getting some sleep at night and not having to constantly tend to a typical campfire. This method of creating a fire utilizes the power of gravity to feed the fire fresh logs. These logs are stacked over one another on two small ramps that roll the logs into one another. The ramps are held up by two large braces, and the whole structure is bound together by paracord.

What You'll Need

- ❖ 4 small tree trunks or large straight tree branches (about 5 ft. in length)
- ❖ 4 branches or smaller trees that will support the larger branches
- ❖ 2 branches about 2 ft. long that will be used in your bracing structure
- ❖ 8 large, 3-ft.-long sections of tree trunk, preferably hardwood
- ❖ 2 small pieces of wood to space your starting logs
- ❖ 50 yards of 50/50 cord
- ❖ Plenty of dry kindling
- ❖ A shovel

The first step in the process is to gather your materials to build the structure itself. Be sure that the materials you gather or cut down are sturdy and strong as this structure will be holding some serious weight.

Look for similar-sized tree trunks or freshly fallen trees to create the V shape that will be filled with your fuel for the fire.

How to Build the Self-Feeding Fire Quickly

You will start by creating the braces using your four smaller branches and your 2-ft. branches.

They will be lashed together with your paracord.

Create two of these braces. One for each side of the structure. The X's mark where the wood should be lashed together

Lash the four larger tree trunks two to each brace. These become the ramp on which your fuel will sit and roll.

For maximum stability be sure to bury each brace underground. Add your logs to the ramps.

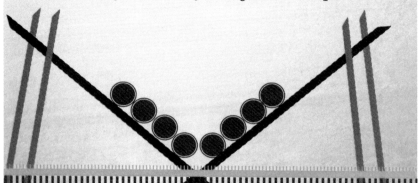

Be sure to space your first two logs with a couple smaller sticks before filling in the kindling areas. This will create critical airflow.

Kindling

To light the fire, place your kindling in the area marked kindling above. Do not remove the spacers that you have put in place. Allow them to burn away as well. Success with your kindling will mean that your first two logs are burning tight against one another. It may not be a roaring flame, but there will be an assuring orange glow that will burn for hours.

If your fire smolders out before the main logs start burning, all is not lost. The quick fix is to space your logs again with a couple new sticks and fill the areas with new kindling again. We are not pioneers nor are we left to their challenges, so if you are really struggling, help this thing along with some kind of accelerant.

The self-feeding fire will easily burn for 8+ hours, allowing you a great sleep without stoking flames and adding logs. This forgotten skill is a testament to what the human race is able to derive from adversity. It's not as easy as throwing together a quick campfire, but I can promise you when you wake up warm to the sun creeping over the horizon and a fire still burning for breakfast, it will all be worth it.

Tips

- ❖ Build your base of sturdy materials, and don't skimp on your paracord.
- ❖ Be sure to bury all of the legs of your structure that touch the ground.
- ❖ The early stages of the fire will be all about oxygen, so provide airflow.
- ❖ Use several sizes of kindling, and distribute it through the length of the first two logs.
- ❖ When in doubt, use an accelerant!

HOW SAILORS FROM THE 17TH CENTURY PRESERVED WATER IN THEIR SHIPS FOR MONTHS ON END

- By S. Walter -

"We never know the worth of water till the well is dry."

— Thomas Fuller, 1732

There is an old Slovakian proverb that goes something like this: "Water is the world's first and foremost medicine." It couldn't be more right.

Between the 16th and 19th centuries, sailing ships dominated naval warfare and international trading routes at sea. Throughout this period, the square-rigged ships carried early settlers, colonizers, and European explorers to different parts of the world, marking one of the world's most widespread human migrations in history. Nicknamed the "Age of Sail,"[1] this period began in 1571 with the Battle of Lepanto and ended in 1862 with the Battle of Hampton Roads when the steam-powered CSS Virginia destroyed the USS Congress and USS Cumberland sailing ships.[2]

European and the American colonies shared a very strong connection between the 16th and 19th centuries—shipping. Back then, sailors would spent weeks, even months, at sea and had to come up with a way to preserve fresh water.

In 1568 the daily ration of water in the Spanish navy was 0.25 gallons. Wine might have been an excellent source of extra calories, but it dehydrated the body. Some didn't even drink their wine. They saved the wine to sell it afterwards upon arrival in America.[3] In 1636 the Admiralty of Amsterdam allowed ships with 100 sailors on board to carry 35 barrels of beer as well, apart from food.[4]

When Jamaica was conquered in 1655, rum became widely available. It was cheap, and sailors soon realized that it lasted better in wooden barrels than beer did. Until 1740 sailors drank the rum in plain form with the permission of the captain. But then the Admiralty demanded for it to be mixed with water, producing a famous beverage called "grog." On extended voyages at sea, sailors needed significant quantities of drinkable water. However, the casks they always had on board were never enough to keep the crew hydrated. To fix the shortage, they would sweeten the water with wine or beer, thus also increasing the gallons available on board. But the wooden casks would often develop algae. Wine and beer spoil pretty quickly, so they came up with a solution: adding rum to the mix. Rum didn't just increase the water amount. It was also used to purify the water. Sixteen ounces of rum (one pint) is enough to purify one gallon of water.

Even though the practice didn't stick in the Royal Navy, it has proven to be a viable alternative for disinfecting contaminated water. If the taste doesn't quite match your preferences, try adding two tablespoons of sugar to the blend or some lemon juice (about 30 ounces). The alcohol in the rum kills harmful pathogens and bacteria, thus making the water you have available safe to drink without getting drunk.

However, even though alcoholic beverages were preferred by the sailors, over-indulgence would often lead to crew impairment in discipline and performance. On top of that, it was a lot more expensive than water. A ship sailing for three months would require about one gallon per day per person, for 135 men. The daily consumption would fluctuate depending on combat circumstances, desertion, disease, and air temperature.

Before there were long-term settlements, our ancestors would often set up camp or stay in a place where there was a nearby water source.

Long Term Water Storage

In 1630 sailors would store their water in wooden casks. They soon realized that casks leak and rot, thus leading to the accumulation of algae and bacteria. As a countermeasure, they started painting and charring casks on the inside before using them. Sulfurization was another practice used to kill bacteria. This involved burning sulfur inside the barrels and generating sulfur dioxide.[5] In spite of the heavy smell—often associated with rotten eggs—the water was safe to drink.

Chlorinating the water is probably the simplest method to get rid of the unpleasant rotten egg smell. However, make sure to use regular bleach only (16 drops - 1/4 tsp - of 6% bleach per 2 gallons of water). For chlorine solution made at home with Granular calcium hypochlorite (one heaping teaspoon -approximately ¼ ounce- to two gallons of water) at 0.05% concentration, add one part of chlorine solution to each 100 parts of water (1 pint of the chlorine solution to every 12.5 gallons of water).

The history of using bleach dates back to the 1800s when a British scientist found out that cholera had spread because of a contaminated water pipe. Upon his discovery, John Snow applied chlorine to water, which was as effective as the people hoped it would be. This discovery led to the first government public regulation to install municipal water filters like chlorine. This is the process that you will have to apply if your municipality water does not add chlorine to the water supply:

- ❖ Add two drops of non-scented chlorine bleach to every two liters of water. Make sure that it is a non-additive.
- ❖ Before drinking or using the water, let it stand for 30 minutes.
- ❖ If you still smell the chlorine in the water, let it stand for another 15 minutes.

! Do not use scented bleaches, color-safe bleaches, or bleaches with added cleaners as prescribed by FEMA, as this will contaminate you water.

! Do not use pool chlorine as it is much stronger than laundry or household bleach.

Aside from household or laundry bleach, you can also use chlorine dioxide tablets and water drops. Potable Aqua tablets have been proven effective against bacteria, Giardia, Lamblia, Cryptosporidium, and viruses. AquaMira water treatment drops are EPA-registered, and a single one-ounce bottle of drops can treat 30 gallons of water.

Treating your water with iodine can also ensure clean drinking water. Simply add 12 drops of 2% tincture of iodine per gallon of water. The only important thing to remember is that family and friends that are pregnant or nursing cannot drink water treated with this process.

Distilling is another way to disinfect water. Basically, you heat up the water to the point when it becomes vapor, cool that vapor, and catch the purified water. It will give you the clean water you need with the only disadvantage being that it is a time-consuming process.

If you don't have that much time and money to spend on all the options above, there are ways to filter your water without making use of electricity and technology. This is based on the sand filters that our ancestors used to sanitize the water in the early 1600s and the first water filters in the 1700s that were made of wool, coal, and charcoal.

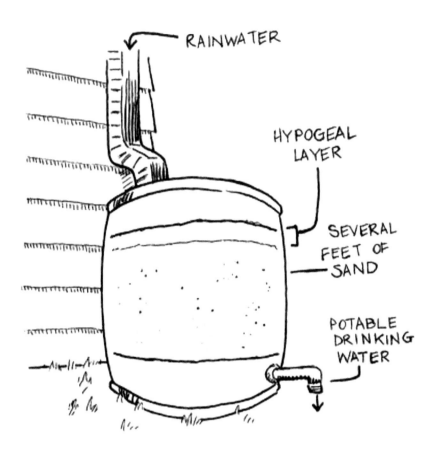

RAINWATER

HYPOGEAL LAYER

SEVERAL FEET OF SAND

POTABLE DRINKING WATER

First, there were sand filters. These use the compact soil and its ability to soak in water. History records that people used to run water slowly and carefully through three to five feet of sand. They would boil the water after that, when they knew that the water was no longer filled with dangerous microorganisms and debris. The important thing to know about sand filters is that the top layer should be cleaned off and replaced regularly.

Today, storing water makes use of different containers. If you're going to use plastic, keep the following thoughts in mind:

- ❖ Not all plastic containers are safe for food and water. Make sure that the outside of your chosen plastic has the recycling symbol with a number in the range of 1 to 7. Be wary of the number 7 however. Although it is food grade just like the others, if the container was not used for any kind of food, do not trust it.
- ❖ The best food-grade containers are those that are marked with the number 2.
- ❖ If you're going to existing plastic containers in your home, do not reuse old milk jugs or cardboard-type juice boxes.
- ❖ Make sure to wash the plastic container thoroughly. If you can't seem to get rid of the smell, do not use it. Follow these steps when you're sanitizing plastic containers like.

Gatorade bottles:

- ❖ Wash each bottle using water and dish soap.
- ❖ Sanitize each bottle and cap inside out with a bleach solution of 1 tsp. bleach mixed in 1 quart of water.
  - ○ Rinse the sanitized bottle with clean water.
  - ○ Fill each bottle with tap water.
  - ○ Add two drops of standard unscented household bleach (4–6% sodium hypochlorite).
  - ○ Empty and refresh your water storage once each year.

Symbol	Code	Material	Examples
♺1	PETE	polyethylene terephthalate	soft drink bottles, mineral water, fruit juice containers and cooking oil
♺2	HDPE	high-density polyethylene	milk jugs, cleaning agents, laundry detergents, bleaching agents, shampoo bottles, washing and shower soaps
♺3	PVC	polyvinyl chloride	trays for sweets, fruit, plastic packing (bubble foil) and food foils to wrap the foodstuff
♺4	LDPE	low-density polyethylene	crushed bottles, shopping bags, highly-resistant sacks and most of the wrappings
♺5	PP	polypropylene	furniture, consumers, luggage, toys as well as bumpers, lining and external borders of the cars
♺6	PS		toys, hard packing, refrigerator trays, cosmetic bags, costume jewellery, audio cassettes, CD cases, vending cups
♺7	OTHER	other plastics, including acrylic, polycarbonate, polylactic fibers, nylon, fiberglass	an example of one type is a polycarbonate used for CD production and baby feeding bottles

❖ If you'd like to be completely safe, the best containers to use are new ones.

If you're going to choose glass containers, here are some guidelines:

❖ Make sure that your glass container is food safe. Some containers may have been used to store chemicals, which could endanger you and your loved ones.

❖ Remember that glass can break easily. It can also crack under freezing temperatures. Worse, it can have tiny, invisible flaws you are unable to see that could trap contaminates in your water. Prepare proper storage.

❖ The best form of glassware that is safe for food and water is Borosilicate glass, more popularly known as Pyrex.

❖ Watch out for soda-lime-based glass that calls itself Pyrex as it is not heat resistant (i.e., Mason jars).

Another form of storage can be stainless steel, which was actually based on the antibacterial properties of silver.

❖ Consider whether or not your water was treated with chlorine. Although stainless steel is actually more durable than the first two options, chlorine alone could corrode the container.

❖ It is better to look for steel drums that are lined a with protective coating to lessen the risks.

❖ As with any container, make sure that your stainless steel containers are food grade.

Filtering Water Supplies

In the early 1800s, sailors began filtering the water. The wooden casks would rot in time, thus affecting the quality of the water. To preserve the freshness, they began adding gunpowder to their putrid water resources. Also known as black powder, gunpowder was made of charcoal, sulfur, and saltpeter (potassium nitrate). An average of three ounces of gunpowder was added to one gallon of water. They would leave the mix to sit for a few hours before consumption.

Sailors didn't know how much gunpowder was needed to freshen the water. They simply checked the level of clarity of the water, the smell, and the taste. If the water didn't smell rotten and the translucency improved, then it was safe to drink. If not, they would add more gunpowder to the mix.

Soon after they realized that gunpowder was a viable solution to make putrid water safe to drink, they began using charcoal. The Japanese were the first to use charcoal to filter water back in the 17th century. Activated charcoal removes chlorine and additional sediments found in contaminated water.

Instructions on How to Make a Charcoal Japanese Water Filter:

❖ Obtain the charcoal—fresh, cooled off, and preferably from a campfire. Remove the ash and dirt, choose the biggest pieces, and crush them into smaller bits

- ❖ Grab a plastic bottle (a regular soda bottle should do) and cut off the bottom—the taller and wider the bottle, the better.
- ❖ Cover the small opening with a piece of cloth (or you can also use grass). Make a small hole into the bottle's cap.
- ❖ Now stuff the crushed charcoal into the bottle. Press tightly.
- ❖ Add another piece of cloth, and press on to the charcoal composition (or you can also use drained sand).
- ❖ Start pouring water, and use another container to gather the filtered water.
- ❖ The water should drip very slowly. If the water doesn't filter slowly, then the charcoal you placed was not pressed tightly enough.

Repeat the process until the water is crystal clear (about two to three times).

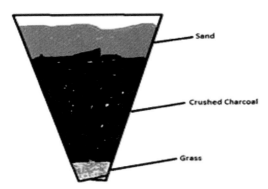

Silver Coins

If silver coins were available on board, sailors would place them in the water barrels to purify the water and kill harmful bacteria.

Silver ions found in silver coins (.999 pure silver, aka colloidal silver) can remove algae, chlorine, lead, bad odors, and bacteria from drinking water. In the 17th century, sailors would spend months at sea. Their water supply was often damaged because wooden casks were perfect for developing rot when coming into contact with moisture. To make the water drinkable again, they would toss silver coins into the barrels. Conventional wooden barrels used by the sailors could fit a quantity of 30 gallons of water per barrel. An average of two silver coins per gallon was enough to purify the water, meaning a whole cask would require an average of 60 silver coins.

The Morgan Dollar coin weighing 26 grams contains 0.7 ounces of pure silver. This means your one coin is enough to purify half a gallon of water.

Casks had a cylindrical shape for easy rolling on the ship. They were made of oak staves and had a bulge in the middle, and iron hoops

were used for tight bounding. Ships carried casks of different capacities (most casks could fit up to 30 gallons of water), and the barrels were placed in the hold to keep the ship balanced.

After consuming the fresh water, sailors would refill the barrels with seawater to preserve the ballast and preserve ship stability. When a ship reached shore, transferring fresh water onto the ship was rather difficult.

Since the water already on board came in casks, emptying the casks (which had to be refilled with seawater to keep the boat balanced) would wreck the boat's ballast. Sailors had to raft the ship with a surf when approaching the coastline. Then they would tow the casks overboard, one by one, and fill them with fresh water from an on-shore pump.

Some sailors used the sailcloth catch system to refill their barrels. They would first wash off the salt accumulated in the casks; then they would taste the water to make sure it was sweet and would then refill their barrels before embarking on another adventure. In extreme circumstances, they would even collect dew (condensed water) from the surface of their ships and drink it to stay hydrated.

Rainwater Harvesting

A great method to stay hydrated at sea required harvesting rainwater. Sailors in the 17th century would catch rainwater by plugging scuppers on the main deck. But in time, they realized that the deck was not a clean environment, and they started using the superstructure of the ship's roof to harvest fresh rainwater. Then they would set up buckets to catch the water or spread a horizontal canvas attached to the rigging and mast. The accumulated water was directed into the casks.

Harvesting Rainwater

People have been harvesting rainwater for centuries, and the techniques and methods used to store it have evolved tremendously. Starting from catching rainwater in large buckets and bins to using more advanced systems, it all depends on the purpose you have in mind for the water that you need. Landowners store rainwater for garden purposes only; other people living in arid parts of the country might want it to survive, or at the very least, they can cut back on expenses on their monthly water bill.

Contrary to popular belief, not all rainwater is safe to drink. It is important to check the pH level of your water before consuming it. (Neutral pH levels are between 7 and 8. Rainwater with a pH level below 7 is acid and shouldn't be consumed until after it has been properly filtered and purified. It may come from the sky, but before reaching the ground, it may come in contact with harmful pollutants in the atmosphere.) If you live in rainy areas of the country, you can easily have one or more barrels (up to 55 gallons) attached to your house's roof pipes.

HOW THE PIONEERS DUG THEIR WELLS TO PROCURE FRESH WATER

- By John Paicu -

"Wisdom prepares for the worst, but folly leaves the worst for the day when it comes."

— *Richard Cecil*

Between the 1700s and the late 1800s, hand-dug wells became extremely popular in North America along the east coast. John Robert Shaw, a famous well digger of the period, dug over 177 wells in four years, totaling 795 meters in depth. He claimed to be very good at locating and digging both fresh water and salt water wells using a method called "water witching," or "dowsing."

The practice involved walking along a property holding a forked stick, a pendulum, and two L-shaped rods to locate the water underground.

The witching rod rotates in the hands of the person walking the property and points toward the ground when a water source is spotted.

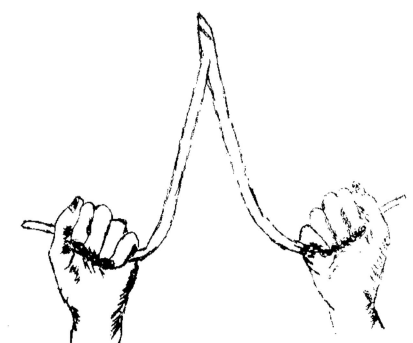

Early settlers dug wells in gravel deposits and sand. They used explosives to achieve the required depth, and then they would carve the hole with rocks to separate the water source from the surrounding ground area.

A well's diameter had to fit the digger, which had to then go down the excavation to drill the holes with a hammer and drill.

Black powder was used to pack the holes, and after lighting the fuse (safety fuses were developed later on, in 1831), the digger had to climb up very quickly, before the well blasted into the rock.

Since lighting a fuse was dangerous, hot coals were thrown into the well to activate the black powder and excite the well.

The black powder was made of an absorbent and nitroglycerin. You'll find the exact procedure together with pictures in *The Lost Ways I*.

Before being used to make dynamite, it was exclusively meant to blast rock. Wells dugs in gravel or sand were lined with brick or cut stone. Cribbing and wood were also common materials used for the lining; however, because wood accumulates humidity and eventually rots, it had to be substituted.

After achieving the desired depth for the well, brick and stone were used from the bottom up to frame the well. At the top, a wooden, brick, or stone curbing was built around the well (four to five feet in height) to prevent debris from going into the well and affecting the quality of the water. For a smoother aboveground curbing finish, mortar was often used as a bucket and windlass base.

In the Western frontier cities, the wells were dug close to stores and in town squares for everyone to access them. The first one was reportedly built in 1839, in Austin, Texas, with a depth of 20 feet. Later on, deeper wells over 250 feet were dug in Western Texan regions. The digging part was done with shovels and picks.

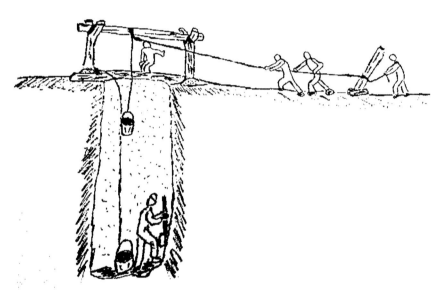

Well drilling technology used by the pioneers

The Chinese were the first to use the percussion method to construct wells. They've been using it for 4,000 years. The wells were dug at staggering depths of 3,000 feet. The percussion system involved frameworks made of bamboo to permit the increase and drop of a heavy crushing or chiseling tool. Today's cable tool rig used for drilling descended from the bamboo framework that the Chinese used to dig their wells.

In America, the first spring-pole well was drilled in 1808, in West Virginia. The depth of the well was nearly 58 feet, and the water was salty. Soon after the discovery was made, the area became a well-known salt manufacturing center. In North America, the pioneers of the drilling method were the Ruffner brothers, who later helped drill the first oil well in the U.S., in 1859.

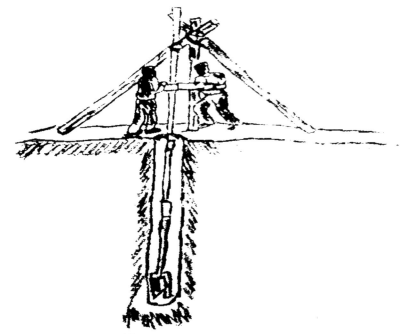

Spring-pole well

Around that same period, many wells were built using the spring-pole. In spite of a simple design, the technique required time and strong legs to be completed. It involved using a long pole, some sort of heavy device to anchor the butt end (e.g., a heavy rock), a stirrup, a fulcrum, oak rods, a manila rope, and downhole tools.

Hemlock was the preferred type of wood for the pole because it was durable.

- ❖ The butt of the pole had to be anchored to the ground using boulders to stabilize the butt. To secure the butt, wooden structures with clamps and a lintel were used.
- ❖ The stirrup was hung by the spring-pole, close to the intended position of the well's borehole, about 3 ½ - 4 feet from the pole's end.
- ❖ The tip of the spring-pole was brought down when the driller pushed it with his leg. Oftentimes two stirrups were added to allow two men to work on the same well.
- ❖ The drill spring (made of a series of vertical tools) was fastened from the pole's end (about 3 feet). The components were oak rods or manila rope, metal connectors, a sinker bar, a rope socket, auger stems, jars, and a bit. The auger stem was a solid iron bar about 3 inches in diameter.
- ❖ Above the borehole, a high tripod had to be erected, and pullies were suspended from the tripod's apex. This maneuver allowed the builders to pull the drill string when changing the tools or when bailing out the hole.
- ❖ A bailer tool was used to retrieve accumulated cavings and cuttings, thus cleaning the well's hole before resuming the percussion drilling process. Later on, the tripod used by the pioneers became the derrick we know today.

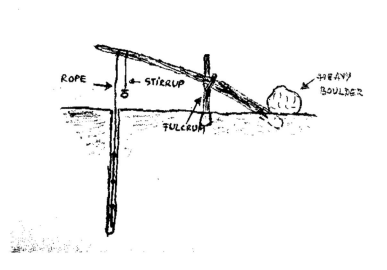

Treadles & Teeter-Totters

In the late 1800s, different arrangements were tried out in an attempt to ditch the leg power used on a spring pole. It was a reliable technique, but it demanded too much strength and endurance. Different "devices" were invented to replace sore legs. However, some seemed a bit too exaggerated. At some point, welders began using horse-powered machines. Horses were placed on a treadmill (usually made of wood), and they were compelled to trod continuously to help operate the walking beam rig.

Steam-Powered Drill Rigs

Steam-powered drill rigs came around the same period. When steam power became available, it started competing with the many walking beam devices. In 1841 the spring pool driller was finally patented. It allowed for many abandoned wells to be reopened. A more sophisticated tool that didn't require a spring pole was made available. It was known as a portable "horse-driven spudder rig." A horse was used to turn the heavy fly wheel, pendulum bar, cam, and elbow lever. All of these combined were meant to drag and drop drilling tools.

The Walking Beam

The history of a walking beam being used to build a well is hazy. Apparently, it became available around the same period as the spring pole, in 1810. Securely sustained by a samson post, the walking beam was developed into a standard device used for cable tool rigging later on, in 1870. It played a fundamental role in the formation of the conventional derrick. Early samson posts were about 10 feet in height. Due to a middle pivot, the center of the beam moved and balanced freely on the post, triggering up and down motions.

How to Dig and Build Your Own Well Like the Pioneers

Early wells dug by the pioneers of the 18th century were basic shallow pits near springs, lakes, and streams. To purify the water, they would use sand, and the well's perimeter was delimited with rocks. Before entering the well, the water had to filter through the sand.

But because the pits were shallow, the water was predisposed to contamination. Soon enough, they started digging deeper wells in search of a more permanent water stream.

Before getting started, you should know that any well has to have a well casing. It is fundamental because it prevents the sides from falling apart (and it guarantees that the water is fresh and bacteria-free). To make your own well, you can even dig the hole yourself with a shovel, use an auger, or use a device such as an excavator to speed up the process.

Step #1: Find a water stream

Find a water stream near your home. Apart from the obvious ravines, assess the vegetation in the area. If you see cottonwood trees, reeds, willows, or cattails, then there's a permanent water stream passing through the ground somewhere. Start digging test pits or holes.

Wait one day to see if the dug area accumulates water. Start digging, and make the pits between 12'' and 24'' deep. In the beginning, the goal is to capture at least a few drops, just to provide some guarantee that you've chosen the right spot. Mark the location where the most water accumulates.

Step #2: Keep digging

Keep digging at a depth between 6 feet and 8 feet. As you dig deeper and deeper into the ground, make sure to shore and mark the sides of the well. Use pieces of lumber as temporary support with an average diameter of 2'' by 6''.

Their purpose is to hold back the walls of the well.

Step #3: Place the flat bricks

After you've reached your desired depth, keep going and over-dig in the middle of the hole. Start placing flat bricks or stones to craft the base. As soon as the base is finished, remove the bottom braces (the temporary support made of lumber). Don't worry if you notice some soil sluffing in.

Use large rocks (river washed) with an average diameter between 6'' and 7'' to make a circle, starting from the bottom up. This will be the first layer of your well's base—the casing. If you can, it might be a good idea to use coarse gravel to backfill the rocks to create even more support for your well's outer wall and to permit the drained water stream to fill your pit.

Step #4: Build the ring of rocks

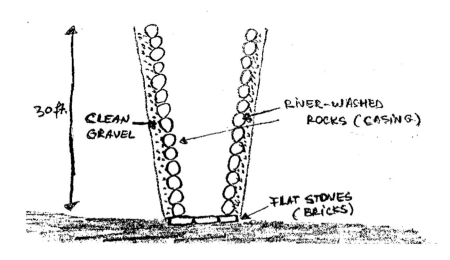

Keep building the ring of rocks until you get to the top, tapering your well's rock wall casing as you go. At the bottom, make is smaller and then slightly larger as you climb up. This technique is two dimensional, and it is meant to provide stability around the wall casing of the well. Basically, you're "encouraging" the water to come from the bottom. Keep digging the pit, and remember to use flat, river-washed stones at the bottom. Coarse the gravel to filter the incoming water.

Step #5: Clean the water

The construction of the walls for your well's casing is done in the same way as for the underground sides. Make sure to block any sort of surface water from entering the well. At the end, before cleaning the well, take a small water sample. Start drawing as much water as you can—the depletion and refilling flushes out lighter materials and sediments so that you have a useable water source. Take another sample.

Toss two cups of chlorine bleach (unscented) into the well, and don't do anything else for 24 hours. Then pump all the water out of the well four more times. If you can still smell the chlorine, keep pumping the water out until the water becomes odorless. Take another sample, and take all three samples for testing to be sure that the water is safe to drink.

EDIBLE PLANTS YOU CAN FIND IN THE WILD

- By Dianne Watkins -

"The time will come that gold will hold no comparison in value to a bushel of wheat."

— By Brigham Young

Before the dawn of agriculture, early man ate a wide variety of wild plants for food, including more than 250 fruits alone. An early study found over a thousand wild plants used by early American Inhabitants. With the development of agriculture, man became less dependent on wild plants and the knowledge of wild plants was not taught.

Scientists have catalogued over 20,000 edible plants, yet most people eat less than 20 different species. In today's tumultuous world, a knowledge of wild foods could be important to survival.

Where to Gather Wild Foods

Start by identifying the common wild edibles in your backyard or in the local parks and botanical gardens nearby. Be careful where you gather plants with the intention of consuming them, use a guidebook and be sure of your identification. Follow these safety guidelines for gathering:

- ❖ Always identify the plant you are gathering. Use pictures and physical characteristics, if you do not have first-hand knowledge of the plant. Take along a field guide whenever possible.
- ❖ Pick only as many plants as you need, and always leave plants behind to replenish the field.
- ❖ Do not eat plants that grow in areas that have been sprayed with chemicals or that grow in polluted waters.
- ❖ Avoid plants that grow near busy roadways, they may contain high concentrations of lead and other harmful chemicals from exposure to car exhaust.
- ❖ Plants growing in contaminated waters should be considered contaminated. Where Giardia lamblia or other parasites are common, boil or disinfect plants before eating.
- ❖ Never gather and eat wild mushrooms unless you are an expert in dealing with mushrooms, it is easy to make a deadly mistake.
- ❖ Do not pick rare or endangered plants.
- ❖ Eat only small amounts of wild plants the first day, increasing your consumption of any one plant slowly. Your system may not tolerate all plants, or you may have unknown allergies.
- ❖ Whenever possible, introduce wild plants to the diet one at a time. This way, if you have a reaction to a plant, you will know which one to avoid.
- ❖ Wash and clean all plants before eating.
- ❖ Never eat any fruit or plant that is starting to spoil or that is growing mildew or fungus.
- ❖ Eat only the plant parts identified as safe.

131

The Universal Edibility Test

In a survival situation, you may not have your field guide to edible plants available, and yet, you need to eat. In such a survival situation, there is a test you can use to determine that a plant or fruit is edible. If you have a reaction at any point during the test, stop the test and choose a different plant or plant part.

Follow these steps:

1. Choose a plant that is abundant in the environment and that you believe to be edible. Test only one part of the plant at a time. For example, test only the leaves.
2. Remove the plant part to be tested from the rest of the plant.
3. Crush the plant and smell it, looking for strong or acid odors, but do not rely on smell alone.
4. Place the crushed plant part on the inside of your elbow or your wrist for 15 minutes. If no skin reaction occurs, you can continue.
5. Wait 8 hours without eating before continuing with the test, drink only purified water. Check your skin again for a rash or irritation. During the test do not eat or drink anything other than the test plant and purified water.
6. Prepare a small portion of the plant part and prepare it for eating. It is usually best to start with a cooked portion. Some plants have toxins that are easily destroyed by cooking, If you are unable to cook it, you can continue to test it raw.
7. Touch a small portion of the prepared plant to your lip and hold it there for 3 minutes, watching for any burning, itching or any other irritation.

8. If there is no reaction after 3 minutes, put the small sample on your tongue and hold it there, without chewing or swallowing, for 15 minutes.

9. If there has been no reaction, chew the portion thoroughly and hold it in your mouth for another 15 minutes without swallowing.

10. If you still have not experienced any burning, itching, numbing, stinging or irritation of any kind, swallow the small portion, but only that one small bite.

11. Wait another 8 hours without eating. If you have any ill effects during the wait time, induce vomiting and drink plenty of water.

12. If you have no reaction to the first bite, eat a small portion of the plant, approximately 1/4 cup, prepared in the same way and wait another 8 hours. Again, induce vomiting and drink plenty of water if you experience any ill effects.

13. If there is still no reaction to the plant, consider the tested plant part safe to eat as prepared. Other parts of the plant will need to be tested in the same way before eating. Increase amounts eaten slowly. Remember that large portions of an unfamiliar plant can cause diarrhea, nausea or cramping on an empty stomach, so eat even safe plants in moderation.

Acorns and the Oak Tree, *Quercus* and *Lithocarpus*

4

Identification. There are about 600 species of oak trees and shrubs. The trees are either deciduous or evergreen with spirally

arranged leaves and leaves with lobate or serrated leaves. A few species have leaves with smooth margins. Acorns are the nut of the oak tree. The edible nut is covered in a cup shaped shell containing a single seed and topped with a cap.

Edibility. Acorns have traditionally been used as forage for pigs, but they are also edible for human use. Gather acorns in the fall and store them whole in a cool, dry place for use throughout the winter. Because acorns contain bitter tannins, which can hinder digestion,

---

4 Photo by David Hill - CCA 2.0

they need to be cracked, chopped and soaked in several changes of water before eating. Soak them until the water no longer turns brown, then cook or dry for use as a flour. Acorns can also be used as a coffee substitute.

As a Remedy. Oak has been used as a medicine to treat bleeding, swelling and dysentery. It functions as a diuretic and as an antidote for poison. Dried and powdered root controls bleeding, reduces swelling and prevents infection. Powdered root was also uses as a snuff to treat tuberculosis. Poultices or compresses made from the leaves promote wound healing, treat rashes, irritations and reduce swelling.

Amaranth, *Amaranthus Retroflexus*

Identification. Amaranth is an edible weed common to most continents. Densely packed flowers grow on stems during the summer or autumn. There are over 60 species of amaranth with red, purple, green or gold flowers.

Edibility. All parts of the plant are edible, but watch for small spines that appear on some leaves. Like many greens, amaranth leaves contain oxalic acid, so it is recommended that you boil the leaves if you are eating them in quantity or often. A few raw leaves in a salad is safe. Harvest amaranth seeds to make a gluten-free grain that is easy to harvest and cook like rice.

As a Remedy. The amaranth seed contains squalene, notable for its anticancer and antioxidant agents. Squalene is estimated to have three times the antioxidants as vitamin C. The leaves, grain and oil of Amaranth, eaten regularly, have been shown to protect the body from cardiovascular disease and helps to lower blood pressure naturally.

Asparagus, *Asparagus Officinalis*

Identification. The same asparagus that we pay dearly for at the supermarket also grows wild. Wild stalks are usually much thinner than the supermarket vegetables, but they can be used in all the same ways.

Asparagus is a perennial, herbaceous plant with many stems, feathery foliage and bell-shaped white to yellow flowers.

Edibility. Gather young asparagus shoots in the spring, before the leaves begin to open. The shoots turn woody as the leaves appear. Eat them raw, steamed, or boiled.

As a Remedy. The leaves and the shoots have a cleansing effect on the digestive system, kidneys and liver. The roots are used as a diuretic and laxative and can reduce blood pressure. They are also used to relieve symptoms of dropsy, gout and rheumatism. The powdered seeds can be used as an antibiotic or to relieve nausea.

Autumn Olive, *Elaeagnus Umbellata*

Identification. Autumn Olive is an invasive shrub in the central and eastern United States. It is often found in old fields and on roadsides. It is identifiable by the small silver speckles covering the leaves and berries.

Edibility. In the fall, the autumn olive produces an abundance of edible red berries. While the berries are edible raw, they are very sour. The flavor is greatly enhanced by cooking them with sugar.

The seeds can be eaten with the berries, either raw or cooked, however the seed coating is very fibrous. The berries can be dried for use as a tea. The leaves and flowers can be used to make a tisane. Since little research has been done on this plant, it is advised that pregnant women avoid it.

As a Remedy. Autumn olive is currently being investigated for its ability to prevent and reverse the growth of cancers. The flowers are astringent and used as a cardiac tonic and as a stimulant. The seeds are used to treat a cough, while oil pressed from the seeds is used to treat lung problems.

Beech, *Fagus Grandifolia*

Identification. The American beech is deciduous, growing 66 to 115 feet tall. The trunk and branches are covered with a smooth, silver-gray bark. Leaves are dark green with serrated edges. [5]

Edibility. The inner bark, young leaves, and the nuts of the American Beech tree are edible. In times of scarcity, beech sawdust

---

[5] Photo by Fritzflohrreynolds – Own Work, CC BY-SA 3.0

has been added to flour to extend it when baking. The sweet seeds are edible raw, but should not be eaten in large quantities because of the fagin content in the skin.

Roasting the seeds allows the skin to be easily removed, along with the offending fagin.

Crush and boil the seeds to make a nourishing drink or grind them to use like cornmeal for baking.

As a Remedy. The leaves and bark are used to reduce inflammation and treat ulcers. The leaves calm the stomach and nervous system. Boiled leaves made into a poultice soothe and heal burns and help repair skin damage from frostbite.

Ground beech nuts have been used as medicine for headaches, vertigo, epilepsy and hydrophobia and for de-worming.

Balsam Fir, *Abies Balsamea*

Identification: The balsam fir is native to eastern and central Canada and the northeastern United States. It is a medium-size coniferous evergreen growing up to 89 feet tall, although most trees are between 46 and 66 feet tall.

The flat needles are dark green and the bark is smooth and grey with resin blisters. It is commonly grown as a Christmas tree in the United States.

Edibility. The inner bark is edible when chewed or cooked. It can be dried and pounded into a powder for use as a flour and thickening agent. Young tips of shoots can be used as a tea substitute.

Caution: Some people are allergic to balsam fir and develop a contact dermatitis when exposed to the leaves.

6

As a Remedy. The bark, needles and resin are common treatments for a variety of illnesses. The needles are high in Vitamin C and useful as a tea to treat poor health, colds, coughs, bronchitis, colic,

---

6 Photo By U.S. Fish and Wildlife Service - Public Domain

asthma, rheumatism, bladder inflammation, sciatica, lumbago, epilepsy, swollen glands, and prevent scurvy.

Smoke from burning needles are useful to treat congestion and headaches. Resin from the bark blisters is used to treat wounds, sores, and skin diseases.

Black Cohosh, *Cimicifuga Racemosa*

Identification. It is also known as black snakeroot, black bugbane, and fairy candle. Black cohosh is a member of the buttercup family native to eastern and central North America.

7

[7] Valérie75 assumed (based on copyright claims). - No machine-readable source provided. CC BY-SA 3.0

It prefers woodland habitats and has star-shaped flowers that grow on stems up to 8 feet tall. The plant has an unpleasant odor which repels insects.

Edibility. Black cohosh is not edible. It is used as an herbal remedy in small doses.

As a Remedy. The roots and rhizomes have been used historically to treat arthritis and muscle pain. Extracts from the plant are analgesic, anti-inflammatory, and act as a sedative. Currently, black cohosh extracts are used as an herbal remedy for menopause symptoms, to treat menstrual cramps, induce labor, and is sometimes used as a hormone replacement therapy.

Avoid black cohosh if you are pregnant or lactating. It can induce miscarriage or harm young children. Women who have or have had breast cancer should also avoid it. Side effects include headaches and skin rashes; extended use can cause liver damage.

Blackberries, Rubus spp.

Identification. Blackberry vines have red branches, long thorns, and wide leaves with jagged edges. The white flowers bloom in the spring and berries ripen in the fall. "Blackberries are red when they are green," so wait until they turn black to harvest them.

Edibility. Use the soft fruit raw or cook it into jams, jelly, desserts or make wine. The roots can be eaten when boiled long enough to soften them. The dried leaves are used in herbal teas. Young shoots of the plant are edible raw if harvested as the first sprout in the spring.

As a Remedy. The root-bark and leaves are diuretic, cleansing, and strongly astringent.

They are used as a remedy for dysentery, hemorrhoids, cystitis, and diarrhea.

Use the roots to make a mouthwash and gargle to treat sore gums, mouth ulcers and sore throats.

The leaves can also be used to make mouthwash and to treat thrush.

Black Locust, *Robinia Pseudoacacia*

Identification. It is also known as false acacia. The deciduous black locust tree is native to the southeastern United States and widely naturalized in other parts of the country. It is also found in Europe, South Africa and Asia.

8

The tree reaches 40 to 100 feet in height in an upright manner. The tree has compound leaves, each containing many leaflets.

Edibility. The bark and leaves of the black locust are toxic, but the flowers are edible. They make a delicately flavored jelly. Shelled seeds are also safe to eat, both raw and boiled.

---

8 Photo By Mehrajmir13

As a Remedy. The flowers are used as a laxative, emollient, diuretic and antispasmodic. Cooked flowers are eaten to treat eye problems. The inner bark and root-bark are emetic, purgative and tonic. Hold the root bark in the mouth to relieve pain from a toothache or chew it to induce vomiting. Juice from the leaves is said to inhibit viruses.

Bloodroot, *Sanguinaria Canadensis*

Identification. It is also known as bloodwort, redroot, red puccoon, and pauson. Bloodroot is a perennial herbaceous flower found in eastern North America. It has variable leaf and flower shapes, but is identifiable by the reddish rhizome with bright orange juice.

Edibility. Bloodroot produces the toxin sanguinarine, which are stored in the rhizome. No part of the plant or root are recommended for internal use. Ingested bloodroot extract can cause nausea, vomiting, headaches, and may lead to a loss of consciousness.

As a Remedy. Bloodroot has been used as a herbal remedy for skin cancer. Applications of bloodroot or its sap to the skin can destroy cells, including cancerous cells. There is no way to determine whether all of the cancerous growth has been eliminated, and the cancer can return. Since some healthy cells are also killed, it can leave ugly scars.

A tea made from the root has been used for sore throats, fever and body aches.

Blueberry, *Cyanococcus, American Blueberry*

Identification. Blueberries grow on upright shrubs of up to 13 feet in height. Leaves can be evergreen or deciduous and the white, pink or red flowers are bell-shaped. The berries are deep blue to dark purple when ripe, usually in mid-summer.

Edibility. Eat the fruit raw or cooked.

As a Remedy. Blueberry juice has been used as a treatment for diseases of the urinary tract and the prevention of cystitis. It also helps prevent or dissolve kidney stones. Blueberries are high in antioxidant compounds and may help protect against oxidative DNA damage of aging and prevent cancer.

They help lower blood pressure and prevent heart disease. Several studies have shown that blueberries, eaten regularly, help improve insulin sensitivity and lower blood sugar levels.

Bull Thistle, *Cirsium Vulgare*

Identification. It also known as spear thistle or common thistle. Bull thistle, a member of the daisy genus, is commonly found throughout North America, Europe, Asia, Africa, and Australia. It is a biennial, forming leaves and a taproot the first year and flowering in the second year.

Edibility. The stems are edible peeled and steamed or boiled. The tap root can be eaten raw or cooked. Harvest the plant in the first year, before it flowers. Once the plant flowers, it is too bitter to be enjoyable.

Use as a Remedy. The roots and plant have been used in a poultice for sore jaws or as an herbal steam for treating rheumatic joints. An infusion of the whole plant has also been used externally or internally as a treatment for bleeding piles.

Bunchberry, *Cornus Canadensis*

9

Identification. It is also known as Canadian dwarf cornel, Canadian bunchberry, quatre-temps, crackerberry, creeping dogwood. Bunchberry is a small, erect perennial that grows 2 to 8 inches tall in the northern United States and Canada. The upper leaves form a

[9] Photo original: JohnHarvey; derivative: Peter Coxhead ,CC BY-SA 3.0

whorl, while the lower leaves are opposite. The fruit are bright red berries in a bunch.

Edibility. Both the fruit and leaves are edible. Eat the fruit raw or cooked, or dry it for later use. Eat the leaves raw or boiled.

As a Remedy. Leaves applied to wounds and sores help stop bleeding and promote healing. The leaves and berries are useful as a treatment for the common cold.

Burdock, *Arctium Lappa*

Identification. Burdock is a medium to large plant with large, dark green leaves and purple, thistle-like flowers. [10]

---

[10] Photo is by Epukas, public domain.

The coarse, oval leaves can grow up to 28 inches long, with lower leaves being heart-shaped.

Edibility. You can eat the leaves and peeled stalks raw or cooked. The leaves taste bitter, but much of the bitterness can be removed by boiling them twice, changing the water each time.

The tap roots are also edible when peeled and boiled. The root is crisp and has a mild, sweet flavor that is improved by soaking the cut roots in water for a few minutes before cooking.

Immature flower stalks can be harvested and eaten in the late spring, before the flowers appear. The taste is reminiscent of artichoke, a relative of burdock.

As a Remedy. Dried burdock is considered a diuretic, diaphoretic and blood purifier. Oil from the root is used as a scalp treatment. Taken internally, it increases circulation to the skin, helping to detoxify it and treat skin abscesses, acne, carbuncles, psoriasis, eczema and similar skin diseases. Burdock root is also good for helping in cellular regeneration, treatment of Crohn's disease and diverticulitis, treatment of Hepatitis, and Chronic Fatigue Syndrome.

Burdock is high in inulin, a carbohydrate that is helpful for diabetes and hypoglycemia.

Cattail, *Typha*

Identification. Usually found near freshwater wetlands, cattails are semi-aquatic perennials with hairless flat blade leaves and a unique flowering spike. The plants grow to heights of 3 to 10 feet.

In some areas, cattails are considered endangered and it is illegal to pick them and in others they are considered invasive. Know your local laws before you plant or harvest this edible plant.

Edibility. The cattails spikes, roots, leaves and stems are edible. The corn-dog like flower spikes are eaten raw like corn on the cob. Boil the leaves before eating. The roots and stems can be eaten raw or boiled.

As a Remedy. Cattail has natural antiseptic properties. A jelly-like substance found between young leaves can be used on wounds, boils, sores and rashes, and as a powerful analgesic taken internally or used topically to relieve pain and reduce inflammation. The plant has coagulant properties, aiding in blood clotting and providing relief from menstrual bleeding.

Clover, *Trifolium*

Identification. Clover can be found in most open grassy areas. They are small ground cover plants, easily recognized by their distinctive trefoil leaflets. Most clover will grow in sets of three leaves, but consider yourself lucky if you find sets of four, and sets with more leaves have been noted.

Edibility. You can eat clover leaves and stems raw or boiled.

As a Remedy. Red clover has been used to treat cancer, whooping cough, respiratory problems and skin irritations. It is known to contain isoflavones which have estrogen-like effects in the body and have shown potential in the treatment of hot-flashes, and other menopause symptoms.

White clover leaves are used in a tea to treat coughs, colds, and fevers. Tea made from the flowers treat rheumatism and gout.

Chicory, *Cichorium Intybus*

Identification. It is also known as also known as blue daisy, blue dandelion, blue sailors, blue weed, bunk, coffeeweed, hendibeh, horseweed, ragged sailors, succory, wild bachelor's buttons, and wild endive.

Chicory grows as a small perennial, herbaceous bush with blue, lavender or white flowers. The stem is tough, hairy and grooved when flowering and grows to be up to 40 inches tall. The leaves are shaped like a lance tip.

Flowers appear from July until October and are usually blue, but occasionally pink or white.

Edibility. The entire plant is edible, but the leaves are bitter. Reduce the bitterness by boiling them and discarding the water. Use the leaves raw or boiled. The roots are tasty boiled and make a good substitute for coffee when roasted and ground.

11

As a Remedy. Root chicory is effective against intestinal worms and internal parasites. Chicory flowers are used as a folk medicine as a tonic and as a treatment for gallstones, stomach upsets, sinus problems and cuts and bruises. A poultice of the roots is useful against chancres and fever sores. It contains inulin, which may help with weight loss and helps in blood sugar regulation in diabetics.

---

[11] Photo By Lmmahood

Chickweed, *Stellaria Media*

Identification. It is also known as chickenwort, craches, maruns, and winterweed. Chickweed sprouts in the late fall or winter, then grows large matts of plants. Leaves are opposite and oval. The plant produces small white flowers with lobed petals.

12

There are several closely related plants which are not edible, but *Stellaria media* is easily distinguished from related plants by a close examination of the stems. Edible chickweed has fine hairs on only

12 By Kaldari - Own work, CC0,

one side of the stem and on the sepals. Inedible species have fine hairs covering the entire stem.

Edibility. Chickweed leaves are eaten raw in salads or boiled as a leaf vegetable. The plant contains saponin, which can be toxic when eaten in large quantities.

As a Remedy. Used as an herbal remedy to cool and soothe itchy skin and treat pulmonary diseases. It's high iron content makes it a valuable treatment for iron-deficiency anemia. It is used to treat skin diseases, rheumatic pains, arthritis and menstrual cramps. A tea made from stems can be applied externally to treat bruises and aches and pains.

Chufa Sedge, *Cyperus Esculentus*

Identification. Chufa sedge, also known as nut grass, yellow nutsedge, tiger nut sedge or earth almond, is a sedge grass native to most of the Western Hemisphere, Southern Europe, Africa, the Middle East, Madagascar, and India. It has become naturalized in many other parts of the world. Chufa is an annual or perennial plant that grows up to 3 feet tall.

Chufa has triangular stems that bear slender leaves and spikelets with flat, oval seeds, surrounded by four hanging bracts. The plant is very fibrous and is often mistaken for a grass. Chufa is valuable for its edible tuber, called tiger nuts or earth almonds. The roots are extensive, with scaly rhizomes and small edible tubers.

Edibility. The tubers have a slightly sweet, nutty flavor. They are hard and require soaking in water to soften them before eating. Grind them into a flour for baking or to make tiger nut milk. The tuber is high in fats, starch, and protein and makes an excellent food source.

As a Remedy. Chufa tubers have been used as a treatment for intestinal worms and bloating. It is a powerful uterine stimulant and is also used as an antidiarrheal, aphrodisiac, digestive treatment and tonic. Chufa milk is packed with nutrients and vitamins that support healing and protect the skin.

Cleavers, *Galium Aparine*

Identification. Cleavers, also known as goosegrass, clivers, catchweed, stickyweed, sticky willy, sticky willow, and robin-run-the-hedge, are an annual that grow along the ground, attaching themselves with small hooked hairs on the stems and leaves. Tiny white to greenish star-shaped flowers appear in early spring to summer in clusters of two or three. Leaves are arranged in whorls of six to eight.

Edibility. Some people get an unpleasant rash from contact with cleavers and should not eat it. For most, Gallium aparine is edible. Gather the leaves and stems before the flowers appear and use them as a cooked vegetable. Dry and roast the fruits for use as a coffee substitute.

As a Remedy. A poultice made from cleavers is used on wounds, ulcers, seborrhea, eczema, psoriasis, and other skin problems. An infusion made from the plant is used to treat glandular fever, tonsillitis, hepatitis, cystitis, and urinary problems.

The juice has a mild laxative effect and is a diuretic. Fresh or dried cleavers is anti-inflammatory, astringent, cleansing, and tonic. It relieves constipation and induces sweating.

Crab Apples, *Malus*

Identification. Crab apples, also known as wild apple, are compact ornamental trees that grow wild. The genus contains up to 55 species of small deciduous apple shrubs and trees native to the temperate zone of the Northern Hemisphere.

Edibility. The fruit is a smaller, more sour version of the domestic apple. Eat them raw or sweeten them to make applesauce, pies, jelly and juice. The leaves can be used to make a tasty tea.

As a Remedy. Many parts of the crab apple tree are used as herbal remedies: The fruit is astringent and useful as a laxative. A poultice made from crushed fruit helps heal inflammations and wounds. The root-bark is useful against worms and parasites and as a sleep inducer. A root-bark infusion is used in the treatment of fevers.

The leaves contain antibacterial agents. Seeds of the crab apple contain toxic hydrogen cyanide which has been claimed to be beneficial in the treatment of cancer, but they are poisonous in large quantities.

Curled Dock, *Rumex Crispus*

Identification. Curled dock grows wild in Europe, North and South America, and Australia. It is recognizable by its tall red stalks, reaching up to 3 feet in height. Smooth leaves grow from a large basal rosette with wavy or curled edges. Flowers and seeds grow in clusters on the stem.

Edibility. Peel and eat the stalk raw or boiled. The leaves are best boiled in several changes of water to remove their bitterness and oxalic acid. Harvest curled dock while young, the mature plants are much too bitter.

As a Remedy. Curled dock has been used as a gentle laxative for the treatment of mild constipation. It has cleansing properties and is used internally to treat diarrhea, piles, bleeding in the lungs, and chronic skin diseases.

A poultice or salve made from the roots is used on wounds, sores, ulcers, and other skin problems. The root can also be dried and applied as a powder.

Dandelion, *Taraxacum Officinale*

Identification. This common weed has very small yellow to orange flowers growing together on a composite flower head and appearing to be one flower.

The leaves are 2 to 10 inches long lobed and grow in a basal rosette from the taproot. Both the stems and leaves produce a sticky white, milky sap when broken. The seeds form a puff ball which is easily dispersed by the wind.

Dandelions are very similar to catsear, and can be distinguished by their unbranched, hairless, leafless, and hollow stems which hold only one flower.

13

---

[13] Photo By Greg Hume - Own work, CC BY-SA 3.0,

Edibility. The entire plant is edible, including the roots. Young leaves are tender, but they develop a bitterness as they mature. Boil them in several changes of water to reduce the bitter taste.

Boil the roots to eat and drink the cooking water as dandelion tea. Eat the flowers raw as a garnish on your salad. Dandelions are also used to make wine.

As a Remedy. The dandelion is a common herbal remedy, effective as a cleansing agent, diuretic, laxative, tonic and as a potassium supplement. All parts of the plant can be used, but the root is most effective. It is also used to purify the liver, treat gallstones, urinary problems, skin diseases, gout, jaundice, and stomach upsets.

Elderberries, *Sambucus*

Identification. Elderberry shrubs grow to be 10 to 25 feet tall. The leaves are round with serrated edges. Identify the plant in the spring by the white flowers and harvest berries in the fall. Ripe berries can be black, red, white or yellow, depending on the species.

Edibility. The elderflower blossoms and cooked elderberries are edible. Syrup made from the elderflower blossoms is used as a flavoring agent or diluted to make a drink. A fermented drink is also made from the flowers.

Berries must be cooked, and are eaten in pies or coated in batter and fried. Uncooked berries and other parts of the plant are poisonous.

As a Remedy. Black elderberry is used medicinally as a treatment for colds, flu, and allergies by reducing the swelling in mucous membranes and relieving congestion. It is also applied to the skin to treat wounds. Elderberry contains antioxidants and may have anti-inflammatory, antiviral and anti-cancer properties.

Fiddleheads, *Matteuccia Struthiopteris*

Identification. Fiddleheads, also known as Ostrich ferns, grow in damp areas of North America in the spring.

 Some other species of ferns are also edible, but check your species before eating. Fiddleheads are the fronds of a young fern, harvested early, while the frond is still tightly curled.

Edibility. Only the closed fiddleheads are edible. Cut them close to the ground, remove the brown husk, and wash them well. Boil them for 15 minutes or steam them for 10 to 12 minutes to kill microbes that they sometimes harbor.

As a Remedy. Fiddleheads have antioxidants and are a valuable plant source of omega-3 and omega-6 fatty acids. An infusion can be gargled to relieve a sore throat.

Leaves from the ostrich fern can be applied directly to the skin to treat wounds, infections and boils.

Field Pennycress, *Thlaspi Vulgaris*

Identification. Field pennycress grows wild in most parts of the parts of the world from early spring to late winter. It is a flowering plant in the cabbage family, Brassicaceae.

Edibility. The seeds and leaves of field pennycress are edible either raw or boiled. Be careful where you harvest field pennycress because it accumulates minerals and heavy metals from the soil. Do not eat field pennycress grown in contaminated soils or near the road.

As a Remedy. Pennycress is used as a treatment for rheumatic disease and as a diuretic. The seeds are anti-inflammatory and useful for the treatment of fluid in the lungs, and fever. The entire plant has anti-bacterial activity and is useful as a blood tonic, as an expectorant and a liver tonic. It is useful in treating carbuncles, accute appendicitis, intestinal problems, menstrual problems, endometriosis, and post-partum pain. Use pennycress with caution; large doses can cause nausea, dizziness and a decrease in infection-fighting white blood cells.

Fireweed, *Epilobium Angustifolium*

Identification. Found primarily in the Northern Hemisphere, this pretty, flowering plant is easily identified by its purple flower and the unique structure of the leaves. The veins in the leaves are circular, rather than running to the edges of the leaves.

Edibility. Eat the leaves of fireweed when they are young and tender or use them to make tea. Mature leaves are tough and bitter. The stalk, flowers, root and seeds are also edible. Scrape and roast the root for a tasty, but sometimes bitter root vegetable.

As a Remedy. Fireweed is used to treat pain and inflammation, reduce fevers and heal wounds. It is also used to treat tumors and enlarged prostate. It is considered a tonic and an astringent.

Foxglove, *Digitalis Purpurea*

Identification. Foxglove is a genus of approximately 20 different plants and shrubs. The plant is often grown as an ornamental for its vivid tulip-shaped flowers. During the first year, only the stem and leaves are produced, and the plant flowers during the second year.

Edibility. The plant is considered poisonous and should be used as a medicinal only under medical advice.

As a Remedy. Digitalis is used as a treatment for atrial fibrillation, a common irregular heart rhythm, and is prescribed, under the drug name digoxin, for heart failure. The dried leaves are used, but taken in excess they can be deadly. An overdose will quickly induce vomiting and nausea to prevent the patient from consuming more. **Foxglove should be used with care only on the advice of a medical professional**.

Garlic Grass, *Allium Vineale*

Identification. Garlic grass, or wild garlic is a perennial species of the wild onion. The plant has a strong garlic odor and flavor.

Edibility. Use it as you would garlic. The leaves are edible raw or cooked. The bulb is small, but very flavorful.

As a Remedy. Allium vineale is an anti-asthmatic, blood purifier, diuretic and expectorant. In children, it is used to treat colic and croup. Eat the raw root to reduce blood pressure and ease shortness of breath. A tincture is used to treat worms. Garlic grass contains sulphur compounds which help reduce cholesterol levels and act as a tonic for the digestive and circulatory system.

Garlic Mustard, *Alliaria Petiolata*

Identification. Garlic mustard, also known as Garlic Mustard, Garlic Root, Hedge Garlic, Sauce-alone, Jack-in-the-bush, Penny Hedge and Poor Man's Mustard, is a biennial flowering plant with clumps of slightly wrinkled leaves that smell of garlic.

Edibility. The flowers, leaves, seeds, and root can be eaten. For best flavor, harvest leaves in the spring; they grow bitter as the weather gets hot. Harvest the horseradish flavored roots in the early spring or late fall.

As a Remedy. The leaves and stems of garlic mustard are useful in treating wounds. They are high in Vitamin C and are used internally to induce sweating and treat bronchitis, asthma and eczema.

Externally, use it as an antiseptic poultice to treat itching of bites and stings, promote wound healing, and treat ulcers and skin problems.

An infusion of roots in oil can be used to make an ointment that relieves bronchitis when rubbed on the chest.

Gooseberry, *Ribes*

Identification. Gooseberry, also known as amla, is found in Europe, Africa, Asia, and in scattered locations in North America. Bushes grow up to 5 feet tall. Branches are grey with long red thorns. Leaves have 5 lobes with rounded edges.

Edibility. The fruit ripens in late spring to early summer. Ripe fruit may be white, as in the photo above, or red. Gooseberries are edible, but very sour. While they can be eaten raw, most people prefer them in jellies, jams, pies, or other preparations that contain sugar. The fruit can also be pickled or dried.

As a Remedy. Gooseberry, eaten daily, has proven benefits for the control of blood sugar in diabetics (eaten without sugar) and pre-diabetics. It enhances food absorption, supports a healthy heart, fortifies the liver, balances stomach acid and improves mental function.

It is high in Vitamin C and a powerful antioxidant. The leaves are used in many hair tonics to enhance hair growth and add shine. A paste of pounded or dried and ground leaves can be applied directly to the scalp and roots of the hair.

Indian Cucumber Root, *Medeola Virginiana*

Identification. Indian cucumber root is a member of the lily family that grows in the forests of the eastern United States. Shoots produce two layers of whorled leaves, the second growing in when the plant flowers. The lower leaves have between five and nine lance shaped leaves, while the upper leaves have three to five ovate leaves. Yellow-green flowers appear in the late spring, followed by dark blue to purple inedible fruit.

Edibility. The plant and berries are not edible. The edible tuber has the smell, taste and crispness of a cucumber.

As a Remedy. The crushed and dried leaves and berries make an infusion that has been used as an anticonvulsive. The root is a diuretic and a laxative.

Green Seaweed, *Ulva Lactuca*

Identification. If you live near the ocean, look for fresh green seaweed in the water. Rinse it with fresh water, if possible and let it dry.

Edibility. Use it raw or cook it in a soup.

As a Remedy. Eating seaweed daily is considered to have many healing benefits. Seaweed is rich in iodine and is helpful in the treatment of goiter and thyroid problems.

It is also high in potassium, and is beneficial as a supplement and as a beneficial supplement for fibromyalgia, exhaustion, anxiety and depression. *Because it is high in iodine, it is useful in preventing the adsorption of radioactive iodine in a nuclear event.*

Hazelnuts, *Corylus Avellane*

14

Identification. Deciduous Hazel shrubs and trees grow to be 12 to 20 feet tall, with rounded, bright green leaves with double-serrated edges.

Single-sex catkins of flowers arrive very early in spring, before the leaves. Female flowers are very small, with only the bright-red styles visible. Male flowers are pale yellow and several inches long.

Edibility. The nuts of all hazel trees are edible. Harvest them in mid-autumn when the trees drop their leaves and nuts. Eat the nuts fresh or dried as a snack or use them to flavor baked goods.

---

14 Photo by Simon A. Eugster, CC-SA 3.0

As a Remedy. Hazel nuts are a source of vitamin E, the oil is used in the cosmetic industry and as a treatment for infection with threadworm or pinworm in babies and children. The bark, leaves, catkins and fruit are astringent and useful for inducing sweating and reducing fevers. They are also used to treat toothaches.

Hickory, *Carya*

Identification. The tree grows to 50 to 60 feet tall with pinnately compound, spear-like green leaves. The small, yellow-green flowers hang from catkins that appear in the spring. Hickory nuts grow enclosed in a husk which opens at maturity in the fall.

Edibility. Hickory nuts are the edible fruit of the deciduous hickory tree. Eat them raw or cooked and store them over the winter in their shells.

As a Remedy. Small, fresh shoots of the shagbark hickory are steamed to make an inhalant useful for headache relief. Hickory bark tea has been used to treat rheumatism and externally in a poultice on rheumatic joints.

Jerusalem Artichoke, *Helianthus Tuberosus*

Identification. Jerusalem artichoke, also known as sunroot, sunchoke, earth apple or topinambour, is the tuber of the helianthus tuberosus plant. The plant has rough, hairy leaves that alternate on the lower part of the plant, but are opposite on the upper part of the stem. The elongated tubers resemble ginger root.

179

Edibility. The tubers are a crisp addition to a slaw or salad eaten raw. Roasted tubers are used as a coffee substitute. They store well in a cool place and become sweeter with storage.

As a Remedy. Jerusalem artichoke is used as an aphrodisiac, diuretic, laxative, as a stomach remedy and general tonic. It is a folk remedy for diabetes and rheumatism.

Japanese Knotweed, *Fallopia Japonica*

Identification. Considered an invasive plant in parts of the United States, Japanese knotweed looks like bamboo or a giant, reddish asparagus. It grows near waterways in sunny locations.

Edibility. The stalks are edible, and at their best in the spring while they are still soft. The flavor is similar to a sour rhubarb and it can be substituted for rhubarb in recipes.

The plant grows in large clumps and is easy to harvest, but do not eat it raw in excess or over a long period as it contains oxalates. Cooking destroys the oxalates and makes it safe to eat in quantity.

As a Remedy. Japanese knotweed contains powerful anti-oxidants that reduce inflammation. It is an excellent source of resveratrol which is useful for its anti-inflammatory and anti-aging properties. It has also been used to lower cholesterol and prevent cancer. Used externally, it is beneficial for skin problems, burns, and wounds.

Joe-Pye Weeds, *Eutrochium*

Identification. Joe-Pye weed is a member of the sunflower family, sporting purple flowers. It is a perennial, growing to 5 feet tall and flowering from July to September.

Edibility. All parts of the plant are edible, including the root. Harvest the leaves and stems before the flowers open and dry them for future use. Harvest the roots in the fall and make an herbal tea with the fresh flowers.

As a Remedy. The plant has been used as a medicinal to treat a variety of illnesses including fevers, typhus, kidney stones, and other urinary tract illnesses. Decoctions made from the root and flowers are diuretic and tonic. It is also used to soothe the nerves, treat menstrual problems, impotence, indigestion, asthma, coughs, colds and headaches.

Kelp, *Alaria Esculenta*

Identification. Kelp is another seaweed, belonging to the brown algae and found in most parts of the world. It consists of long, flat, blades growing from stem-like stipes.

Edibility. Like green seaweed, eat it raw or use it in a soup.

As a Remedy. Kelp is a valuable source of iodine and is useful to treat goiter and thyroid problems and protects against radiation poisoning. Iodine is important in female hormone regulation and supports the immune system.

It also contains enzymes that help digestion. It has anti-inflammatory benefits and offers therapeutic potential for neurodegenerative diseases. Caution: Some people are allergic to kelp and may experience symptoms such as rashes, hives, itchy eyes, runny nose, shortness of breath, or gastro-intestinal problems.

15

Kudzu, *Japanese Arrowroot*

Identification. If you have kudzu growing near you, it is an almost limitless source of food. Often found climbing over trees, shrubs, even abandoned houses, the plant is fast growing and considered invasive in most areas.

---

15 Bjørn Christian Tørrissen - Own work , CC3.0

Edibility. The entire plant is edible. The roots are starchy and eaten like potatoes, while the leaves are eaten raw or cooked like a green. Jelly or tea is made from the flowers.

As a Remedy. Kudzu is used to treat muscular aches, headaches and migraines, heart disease and angina, allergies and diarrhea. Kudzu should not be taken by pregnant and lactating women.

Lamb's Quarters, *Chenopodium*

Identification. The plant is also known as goosefoot or pigweed and grows in clumps of 6 to 9 feet tall plants. It has pale green, waxy leaves that are whitish on the underside. Caution: Nettleleaf goosefoot is a poisonous plant that looks like lamb's quarter. It can be distinguished by the undesirable odor of nettleleaf goosefoot.

Edibility. Harvest lamb's quarters when the leaves are young, before the flowers appear. If consistently harvested, they can be eaten throughout the summer, until the first frost.

The leaves contain oxalic acid, so eat them raw in moderation or cook them like spinach to destroy the oxalic acid. The leaves can also be dried and powdered to make flour

As a Remedy. Lamb's quarter are high in vitamins and minerals, it is one of the most nutritious wild foods. The plants can be made into a poultice to relieve pain from rheumatism and arthritis and to relieve swelling and inflammation. Chew raw leaves to relieve toothaches.

Mayapple, *Podophyllum*

Identification. Mayapple, also known as American mandrake, wild mandrake and ground lemon, grows wild in most of the eastern United States and southeastern Canada. The plants grow in clusters originating from a single root.

Edibility. The plant is extremely poisonous, including the green fruit. The fruit becomes edible when it is fully ripe and has turned yellow and softened. Remove the seeds before consuming. Be careful when handling the plant; the toxins can be absorbed through the skin.

As a Remedy. Mayapple plant is poisonous and should not be eaten. While it has been used as an herbal remedy and to induce miscarriages, it is easy to overdose and poison the patient.

Mustang Grapes, *Vitis Mustangensis*

16

---

16 Photo by Ddal, CC-SA 3.0

Identification. Mustang grapes, also known as wild grapes, are common along riverbanks and in moist locations throughout the southeastern United States. The vines are woody and produce small cluster of grapes that ripen into dark purple grapes in August to September. The skin of the grape is thick.

The leaves are easily recognized by the white velvet-soft underside of the leaf.

Edibility. The fruit are extremely acidic, but very tasty used in jelly or as a juice, sweetened with sugar. It is also a popular fruit used for winemaking. The leaves are often eaten in "dolmades", cooked and stuffed with a mixture of rice, meat and spices.

As a Remedy. No known use.

Miners Lettuce, *Claytonia Perfoliate*

Identification. It is also known as Indian lettuce, spring beauty, or winter purslane. Look for miner's lettuce in cool, damp conditions. This herbaceous annual grows from a rosette at the base. Small pink or white flowers appear in the early spring to early summer.

Edibility. The flowers, leaves and roots of miner's lettuce are all edible either raw or cooked like spinach.

The young leaves are fairly bland, but the flavor becomes more bitter as the leaves mature.

The roots are also edible raw or cooked. Although small and a chore to harvest, the root bulbs have the flavor of chestnuts when boiled and peeled.

As a Remedy. The plant is rich in vitamin C and can be used as a tonic, diuretic, or a gentle laxative.

A poultice made from macerated plants is used to relieve the pain of rheumatic joints.

Monkey Flower, *Erythranthe*

Identification. Erythranthe, also known as musk flower, is a diverse plant genus. The plants are usually annuals or herbaceous perennials with red, pink or yellow flowers.

They often grow in damp or wet soils.

Edibility. Harvest monkey flower stems and leaves before the flowers appear for best flavor.

The flowers are also good in salads or used as a garnish. Use monkey flower leaves raw or cooked like greens.

As a Remedy. Erythranthe is listed as one of plants used to prepare Bach flower remedies.

Cautions: Monkey flower species tend to concentrate salts in their leaves and stems, so early travelers used them as a salt substitute. Several species of Erythranthe are listed as threatened; investigate your supply before harvesting.

Pecans, *Carya Illinoinensis*

Identification. The pecan is a large deciduous tree, growing up to 100 feet tall. They have alternate leaves, 12 to 18 inches long and pinnate with 9 to 17 leaflets.

Edibility. The seeds, technically a fruit, but recognized as a nut, are edible. Most people are familiar with the pecan nut, but may not recognize it covered by its husk. The husk opens and releases the nut to fall to the ground when ripe. Gather nuts under pecan trees in the fall.

As a Remedy. The bark and leaves of the pecan tree are astringent. A decoction made by boiling the bark was used to treat Tuberculosis. The pounded leaves can be rubbed on the skin as a ringworm treatment.

Persimmon, *Diospyros Virginiana*

Identification. Persimmon trees grow throughout the southeastern United States, usually in open woods or fields. The tree is usually about 15 to 30 feet tall, but can grow to 80 feet, with oval leaves and male and female flowers on separate short stalks. Male flowers grow 16 flowers per stem, arranged in pairs, while female flowers grow a single flower on each stem. The fruit are usually small, about 1/2 inch in diameter and bright orange when they ripen in the late fall.

Edibility. Gather the fruit when they are soft and fully ripe. Eat them fresh or use the pulp in jelly, breads, cakes and pies. You can substitute persimmon pulp in any recipe calling for banana pulp. Dried persimmon leaves make a delicious tea that is rich in vitamin C and the roasted seed is used as a coffee substitute.

As a Remedy. Teas made from persimmon leaves act as a diuretic and help reduce high blood pressure. They are also useful as an anti-inflammatory for arthritis or gout. Infusions or decoctions of the persimmon tree bark have antiviral and anti-bacterial properties and are useful for treating colds, coughs and the flu. Externally the infusions of leaves or root decoctions are used to disinfect wounds and help healing. They can also be applied to reduce pain and inflammation, including the inflammation of hemorrhoids.

The unripe persimmon fruit are very astringent and can be used to treat diarrhea. Eating the ripe fruit helps lower cholesterol.

Pine Trees, *Pinus*

Identification. Pine trees are evergreen conifers growing 10 to 260 feet tall. Most pines have thick, scaly bark, but a few have thin, flaky bark. Branches grow in a tight spiral, producing needles and seed cones.

Edibility. The soft, white, inner bark of all pine trees is edible. It can be eaten raw or dried and ground into a powder for use as a flour or thickener in cooking. Young, green pine needles can be steeped in boiling water to make a tea that is high in vitamins A and C.

All pine trees bear edible nuts, but most are very small. They are a good source of protein, fat, and carbohydrates.

Harvest pine cones at the end of summer or early fall, before the cones have opened. Wear gloves and old clothes, the pine sap causes a sticky mess. Gather unopened or half-opened cones from the tree, pulling them off the tree or knocking them down with a stick. Cones on the ground will usually have already opened and released their nuts.

Pick the nuts out of half-opened cones immediately, then shell them and toast or eat them raw. Put the unopened cones in a burlap or fabric sac with good air flow and hang them outside to ripen. The first freeze will force the cones to open enough that you can pick the seeds out.

If you don't want to wait, bury the closed cones in the ashes of a hot fire and allow the heat to open the cones. Don't try to put them directly into the fire, they burn very hot and can pop, throwing hot nuts onto nearby diners.

As a Remedy. Pine sap is a natural disinfectant and antiseptic with both antimicrobial and antifungal properties. Apply it directly to wounds to stop blood flow and disinfect the wound.

Pineapple Weed, *Matricaria Discoidea*

Identification. Pineapple weed, also known as wild chamomile, and disc mayweed, is an annual in the Asteraceae family, growing 2 to 16 inches tall.

17

---

17 Photo by Krzysztof Ziarnek - Own work, CC 3.0

Cone-shaped flowerheads holding densely packed yellowish green corollas appear from March to September. The crushed flowers have a definite pineapple and chamomile scent.

Edibility. Pineapple weed flowers and leaves are edible raw in salads or brew to make an herbal tea. When crushed, the flowers have the aroma of pineapple and chamomile. The plant has also been used for medicinal purposes to relieve upset stomachs, fever and fight infections.

As a Remedy. Pineapple weed is rarely used medicinally, although it has been used in the past to treat intestinal worms and as a sedative.

Plantain, *Plantago*

Identification. This is not the banana like fruit, but rather a green plant that grows in wetlands, marshes, bogs, and alpine forests.

The oval leaves have vertical ribs and can grow to be up to 6 inches long and 4 inches wide.

Edibility. The leaves are edible at all times, but they grow more bitter as they mature. Use them raw in salads or cook them as a pot herb.

As a Remedy. Plantain roots are used in a wide range of remedies, including: stomach upsets, peptic ulcers, diarrhea, Iritable bowel syndrome, hemorrhoids, cystitis, bronchitis, sinusitis, asthma, coughs, hay fever. It causes a natural aversion to tobacco and is used in smoking cessation programs.

The root is also rumored to be an anti-venom for rattlesnake bites. Heated leaves made into a compress are useful for skin inflammation, wounds, ulcers, stings and inflammation. Ground plantain seeds act as a laxative and are used for the treatment of parasitic worms.

Prickly Pear Cactus, *Opuntia Compressa, Opuntia Drummondi, and Optuntia Vulgaxis*

Identification. Prickly pears are a cactus that grow in the American west and in the coastal plain region of the southeastern United States. They are native to sandy or rocky soil.

Edibility. Prickly pear cactus produce a red or purplish fruit that is covered with tiny spines. You definitely want to wear gloves and handle these fruit with care. The spines are easily removed by securing the fruit in a pair of tongs and holding it over a small flame to burn off the spines. Use prickly pear fruit to make jelly or jam or cook it to extract a nutritious juice.

The green cactus pads, called nopal or nopales, are also eaten. Scrape the bristles off with a knife and trim the pad around the edge. Boil the pads for 10 to 15 minutes and eat them as a vegetable.

As a Remedy. Used fresh, the leaf pars are a diuretic and can be used in a poultice on skin sores and infections. The fruit is packed with anti-oxidants and is anti-inflammatory.

Prunella Vulgaris

Identification. Prunella vulgaris, also known as Self-Heal or Heal-all, grows 2 to 12 inches high with creeping stems that root where they land. The stems are square with leaves growing in opposite pairs. Leaves are elongated with serrated edges and a reddish tip.

Edibility. Self-heal is entirely edible. The young leaves and stems are good raw or the whole plant can be cooked and eaten.

As a Remedy. The plant is used medicinally to make a dressing for wounds, ulcers, sores and other skin problems.

A tea made from the plant was taken to treat fevers, diarrhea, internal bleeding, nephritis, and goiter. The plant is antibacterial and antiseptic and astringent. Use it fresh and harvest it mid-summer and dry it for later use.

Purslane, *Portulaca Oleracea*

Identification. Purslane, also known as verdolaga, pigweed, little hogweed, red root, parsley, is a succulent plant with smooth, flat leaves. It grows from early summer through fall and may grow to 16 inches in height.

Edibility. Eat it raw or boiled. The leaves have a sour taste and contain oxalate, but both are reduced by boiling.

As a Remedy. Purslane is used to treat and prevent a wide variety of illnesses, including cataracts, dysentery, heart disease, asthma, cardiac arrhythmia, intestinal worms, gum disease, multiple sclerosis, psoriasis, stomach aches, headaches and depression.

It is high in vitamins A, C, and E, as well as calcium and magnesium and is thought to boost the immune system.

Red Mulberry, *Morus Rubra*

Identification. Red mulberry trees are native to the eastern and central Unites States. The tree is deciduous, growing up to 70 feet tall. The leaves are alternate with a sand-paper like upper surface.

Edibility. Red mulberry fruit look a lot like ripening blackberries, but they are less tart. Watch for them to ripen in the late spring to early summer.

Pick them as soon as they are ripe, or you will have competition from the local birds.

As a Remedy. Tea made from the root of red mulberry trees is effective against parasitic worms, tapeworms, dysentery, and urinary problems.

The sap is useful to treat ringworm. The fruit helps reduce fevers.

Rose, *Rosaceae*

Identification. Roses are a large family with thousands of cultivars. They grow as shrubs and vines and usually have thorns. Flowers are large and often fragrant.

Edibility. The flower petals and rose hips produced by many garden roses are edible. The petals plucked from open blooms are used to make tea, syrups, rose water, and as a flavoring in foods. Rose hips, the mature seed pods from the rose flower, is used to make jams, jellies, marmalades, soups and teas.

As a Remedy. Rose hips, leaves, petals and roots have been used for a wide variety of remedies including treatment of colds, flu, fevers, diarrhea and stomach upsets.

Rose hips are highly valued for their vitamin C content.

A boiled tea made from the hips or roots has been used to treat eye infections and inflammations.

The FDA has designated the rose flowers, fruit (hips) and leaves of *Rosa alba* L., *Rosa centifolia* L., *Rosa damascena* Mill., and *Rosa gallica* L. as "Generally Recognized as Safe".

Seneca Snakeroot, *Polygala Senega*[18]

Identification. Seneca Snakeroot, also known as Senegaroot or Rattlesnake root, is a perennial herb in the milkwort family. It is named to honor the Seneca people, who used the plant as a treatment for snakebite. The plant grows to be 20 inches tall with many unbranched stems. Lance-shaped leaves alternate with

---

[18] Photo By Rob Routledge, Sault College, Bugwood.org - Image Number 5473588 at Forestry Images, The Bugwood Network at the University of Georgia and the USDA Forest Service., CC BY 3.0

smaller lower leaves. The small, pea-like white or greenish flowers grow on a spike. The root has a scent reminiscent of wintergreen and a pungent flavor.

Edibility. The plant and root are for medicinal use only and are not edible. Large doses are poisonous.

As a Remedy: Seneca snakeroot is most commonly used as an expectorant in respiratory problems such as colds, croup, and pleurisy. Root tea was also used for pneumonia, bronchitis, whooping cough, asthma, and to calm the mucous membranes. The plant is still used as an herbal remedy for respiratory problems.

Root tea is an emetic, induces perspiration, and helps regulate menses. It has also been used to treat rheumatism, heart problems, convulsions, and inflammation.

The Seneca people chewed the root and applied the mash to snakebites after sucking out the poison, hence the name.

Sheep Sorrel, *Rumex Acetosella*

Identification. Sheep sorrel is found in the highly acidic soil of fields, grasslands and woodlands in Europe, Asia, and North America. The plant has a reddish stem that grows up to 18 inches tall and green arrow-shaped leaves.

Identification. Sheep sorrel can be eaten raw, but it contains oxalates, so either cook it or eat only small quantities. It has a tart, lemony flavor. Sheep sorrel can also be used as a curdling agent for cheese making.

As a Remedy. The fresh juice of sheep sorrel is a diuretic and is considered detoxifying. It has a mild laxative effect and is used for stomach problems and to expel worms.

A root decoction has been used for excessive menstruation, stomach ulcers and diarrhea.

A tea from the leaves can be used externally to treat boils, abscesses, sores and other skin diseases. Used as a poultice, the leaves reduce inflammation.

Spikenard, *Aralia Racemosa*

Identification. Spikenard, also known as American Spikenard, Petty Morel, Indian Root, Spice berry, and Life-of-man, is an herbaceous plant, growing up to 4 feet tall in moist soil and semi-shade. It is found mostly in the eastern United States. It bears hermaphrodite flowers in early summer.

Edibility. The fruit, leaves, young shoots, and root are edible, mostly used as a flavoring for its liquorice flavor and for making root beer. It can be eaten cooked as a green vegetable. The fruit are tasty eaten raw or cooked.

19

---

19 Photo By Urban - Own work, Public Domain

As a Remedy. American Spicknard has been used as a healing plant for thousands of years.

The root's antiseptic, diuretic, detoxifying and diaphoretic properties make it useful as a purifier, and to treat a variety of conditions including coughs and respiratory illnesses, rheumatism and gout.

Applied externally as a poultice, it is used to treat skin problems and rheumatism. The roots can be collected in the summer and fall and dried for later use.

Spruce, *Picea*

Identification. The spruce is a coniferous evergreen tree. Branches are whorled and produce needles attached in a spiral form. It is covered with scaly, reddish-brown bark and grows to be from 60 to 200 feet tall. It produces yellow or red male catkin-like flowers and bright purple female flowers in the spring. The resulting seed cones are oblong.

Edibility. All parts of the spruce tree are edible. The needles are used to make a tea, and the inner bark and green cones are palatable, although a little bitter.

For an easy snack, chew on a sprig of new growth in the spring. Spruce is a valuable source of vitamin C during the winter months when little else is growing.

As a Remedy. The young shoots and leaves are most often used medicinally. A tea made from young shoots reduces fevers and promotes sweating. It is used to treat coughs, colds and the flu and the inhaled vapors are used for bronchitis. Use the pitch from spruce trees as an external treatment for wounds, ulcers and sores.

Tea made from shoots or leaves is used for treating bladder infections, scurvy, gonorrhea, and as a general cleansing tonic.

Sunflower, *Helianthus Annuus*, Common Sunflower

Identification. The sunflower is an annual plant in the family Asteraceae, known for its huge flowering head. The plants are annuals or perennials growing to 10 feet tall or more.

The flower heads have bright yellow ray florets around a yellow or maroon disc with florets inside. The plant tilts to face the sun during the day, until the flower is produced, then they usually face east. Seeds are produced on the disc, the ray flowers are sterile.

Edibility. In addition to the popular sunflower seeds, the leaves, flowers and stems are also edible. The seeds are eaten raw or cooked and can be roasted to make a coffee substitute.

Young flower buds are best steamed, while the leaves and stalks can be boiled and served as a green vegetable.

As a Remedy. A tea made from the leaves is used to treat coughs and fevers. Crushed leaves are used on skin wounds, sores, stings and snakebites. A tea made from the flower is used to treat malaria and lung diseases.

Sweet Rocket, *Hesperis Matronalis*

Identification.[20] Sweet rocket, also known as Dame's Rocket, is a member of the mustard family and is known by many names. Often mistaken for Phlox, it's flowers have four petals, while Phlox flowers have five. The plant produces a mound of hairy foliage the first year and flowers in the second spring.

Edibility. Harvest sweet rocket before the plant flowers. Young leaves are best used as salad greens.

Seeds can be sprouted for micro-greens and used in salads.

As a Remedy. Harvest leaves while the plant is flowering and dry them for use as a diuretic and to induce perspiration. They are high in vitamin C and are useful in preventing scurvy.

---

[20] Photo by Gregory Phillips, CC-SA 3.0

Tobacco, *Nicotiana Tabacum*

Identification. Tobacco is an annual herbaceous plant of the Solanaceae family. Some Nicotiana species are cultivated as ornamentals, but most are grown for tobacco leaf production. The plant grows to 4 feet tall and flowers from July to September.

Edibility. While protein extracts can be made from the leaves, it is highly toxic in its natural state, even in small amounts. All parts of the plant contain nicotine, which is the addictive substance in tobacco.

As a Remedy. Tobacco has a long history as a medicinal plant, commonly used as a relaxant. The leaves are used externally to treat skin diseases, scorpion stings and bug stings. Do not ingest the plant, it is an addictive narcotic and extremely toxic.

A homeopathic remedy made from dried leaves is used to treat nausea and motion sickness. The leaves are a diuretic, expectorant, irritant, narcotic, sedative and antispasmodic.

Violets, *Viola Papilionacea*

Identification. Violets are easily identified by the flowers and by their heart shaped leaves.

Edibility. The flowers and leaves both edible. The flowers are often used by chefs as a garnish for salads and cakes, and can be made into a tea or syrup. Similar to spinach in flavor, the leaves are used raw in salads or cooked as a green.

As a Remedy. Violets and their extracts have been used experimentally to treat tumors in mice, but no human trials have been done. The leaves and flowers are beneficial as an expectorant to treat coughs, colds and bronchitis. A tea made from the leaves is beneficial for insomnia and as a laxative.

Violet leaves have also been reported to have antiseptic and pain relieving effects. Use a tea or compress to relieve headaches and neck pain. Use in a poultice or in ointment form to relieve symptoms and heal wounds, sores and skin problems.

Walnuts, *Juglans*

Identification. Walnut trees are deciduous, growing up to 130 feet tall, with pinnate leaves in clusters of 5 to 25 leaflets. Leaves and blossoms appear in the mid-spring and the nuts ripen in the fall.

Edibility. The nuts of the walnut tree are edible and considered a good source of healthy oils and protein. Walnuts can be pickled in vinegar while still green in their husks or allowed to ripen on the tree and eaten shelled as a nut. Store the nuts in a cool, dry place to prevent mold and spoilage. The leaves can be used to make tea, and the sap can be tapped in the spring to make syrup or sugar.

As a Remedy. Walnut leaves are used internally purify the blood and to treat constipation, stomach upsets, nausea, diarrhea, coughs, and asthma.

The nuts and leaves are also used externally to treat skin diseases, eczema, wounds, and sores.

The walnuts are diuretic and a stimulant, and have been used to treat urination problems, back pain, and weakness in the legs.

Oil from the seed is used to treat dry skin and to treat parasitic worms.

Watercress, *Nasturtium Officinale*

Identification. Watercress, a member of the Brassicaceae is a rapidly growing aquatic perennial with a spicy flavor. The stems are hollow and allow the plant to float. If left to grow, it can reach a height of 4 feet. Despite the botanical name, watercress is not to be confused with the nasturtium flowers.

Edibility. Use the leaves and stems raw in salads, sandwiches and in soups. Sprout the seeds for their edible shoots. The leaves are best harvested before the plant begins to flower and the foliage turns bitter. Caution: Watercress grown where manure is present can host parasites, so look for plants grown in clean water.

As a Remedy. Watercress is used to treat respiratory illnesses such as coughs, colds, bronchitis, runny nose, sore throat and fevers. It has diuretic properties that help reduce edema and lower blood pressure.

It has also been used historically to treat metabolic diseases, purify the blood and as a general tonic.

White Mustard, Sinapis alba

Identification. White mustard is an annual that grows over 2 feet high with pinnate leaves. It blooms in the early spring, producing hairy seed pods. White mustard seeds are hard, round seeds, growing approximately 6 to a pod.

Edibility. The seeds, flowers, and leaves are edible. Harvest the seeds as the pods just begin to ripen, before they burst. Use the seeds for pickling or grind them and mix with vinegar to make a mustard condiment. The leaves are edible as mustard greens.

As a Remedy. Mustard seeds are known to be antibacterial, antifungal, an expectorant and diuretic. It mostly used externally as a poultice or added to bath water to treat coughs, tuberculosis and pleurisy. The seeds are an irritant to the mucous membranes and the skin, so dilute it and use it carefully.

Wild Black Cherry, *Prunus Serotine*

Identification. Wild Black Cherry trees, also known as rum cherry, black cherry, or mountain black cherry, grow to 50 to 80 feet. It has dark gray bark with a reddish inner bark. The leaves are lance-shaped with toothed margins. The small white flowers appear from

April to June. Each flower has 5 petals and grows in bunches of several dozen flowers.

Edibility. The edible cherries are reddish-black when ripe. Eat only ripe fruit, but do not eat the overripe fruit on the ground and cook all fruit before eating. The taste is sharper than sweet cherries, but appealing. Use the fruit to make jam, pies, pastries and as a flavoring.

As a Remedy. Steep the bark in hot water, but do not boil. Use it to treat coughs, fevers, colds, flu, whooping cough, bronchial spasms, bronchitis, pneumonia, asthma, laryngitis and sore throats. It is also used to treat high blood pressure and poor circulation, relieve inflammation and reduce edema.

Wild Leeks, *Allium Tricoccum*

Identification. Wild leeks, also known as ramps, spring onion, wood leek and wild garlic, are a perennial plant with broad leaves and a white bulb at ground level.

They grow in closely packed groups and smell like onions and garlic with a flavor to match. Wild leeks look similar to the poisonous Lily -of-the-Valley, so be sure of your identification.

Edibility. Collect wild leeks in the early spring, taking only what you need and leaving the rest to replenish the supply. Eat the leaves and bulbs in salads or cooked. In many places, the harvesting of wild leeks is limited by law, so check your local laws before picking.

As a Remedy. Use wild leeks in the same way you would use garlic or onion for colds, croup and as a spring tonic. The warm juice of the leaves and bulbs is used for earaches.

Wild Potato-Vine, *Ipomoea Pandurata*

Identification. An Herbaceous perennial, the wild potato-vine grows in woodland areas. It is also known as man of the earth, wild potato vine, manroot, wild sweet potato, and wild rhubarb and produces white funnel-shaped flowers (morning-glory) with a reddish-purple throat. The thin, heart-shaped leaves are 3 to 6 inches long. Unlike other morning-glories, it has ridged sepals and an enlarged root that can grow to be several feet long, 5 inches in diameter, and weigh up to 30 pounds.

Edibility. The large tuber is used as a food source or as a medicinal. Roast it to eat like a potato.

As a Remedy. Use the cooked root to prepare a pain-relieving poultice for aching joints. Raw roots are used sparingly as an expectorant, diuretic and laxative.

Wild Plum, *Prunus Americana*

Identification. The perennial wild plum grows as a large bush or small tree, up to 25 feet tall. It is also known as American plum or yellow sweet plum. The tree spreads through the roots, creating groups of the thorny bushes. The alternate leaves are simple and oval or oblong in shape. They are 3 to 4 inches long and pointed at the tip.

Fragrant flowers appear before or with the first leaves in the spring. Fruits are small, approximately 1 inch in diameter, with a single rounded pit.

Edibility. Look for ripe plums in the fall. The fruit is yellow-red to red when ripe. The fruit is sweet and sour, suitable for eating fresh or making preserves, jelly, jam and wine. It can also be dried for later use.

As a Remedy. The bark of wild plum has been used to treat coughs, and to make a tea that treats kidney and bladder infections.

Wild Yam, *Dioscorea Villosa*

Identification. The wild yam, also known as colic-root, Rheumatism root, and Devil's-bones, is a climbing vine common in the eastern United States. It grows in damp locations, including swamps, thickets, damp woods and near ditches.

It has a smooth, reddish-brown stem and heart-shaped leaves with prominent veins running from the top center of the heart to the edges in a fan pattern. The long, branched root is woody and forms tubers with a brown skin and white, fibrous center. [21]

---

[21] Photo by Phyzome assumed (based on copyright claims), CC BY-SA 3.0

Edibility. The tubers are edible, although bland. Gather them in the fall and cook them with seasoning to improve the flavor.

As a Remedy. The tubers of wild yam contain chemicals similar to progesterone, estrogen and steroids used as contraceptives. Components of the plant are used in the chemical manufacture of hormones. A decoction of the root is often used as a natural hormone therapy for PMS, menstrual cramps, symptoms of menopause, and for increasing sexual drive and energy in both men and women. It also has anti-inflammatory and anti-spasmodic properties and acts as a vaso-dilator.

Wintergreen, *Gaultheria Procumbens*

Identification. The American Wintergreen is the shrub originally responsible for the wintergreen flavor used in chewing gum, mouthwashes, toothpaste, candies and other mint flavored foods. Stems of the shrub creep along the soil and send up branches 2 to 6 inches tall. The alternate, oval leaves are leathery with serrated edges. The leaves and the bell-shaped flowers grow near the top of the branches. Flowers appear from spring through summer, with berrylike fruit following. The plant has the taste and scent of wintergreen.

Edibility. The berries and leaves are edible in moderation and are mostly used as a flavoring

As a Remedy. American wintergreen is used medicinally for various aches, pains and fever. The leaves contain methyl salicylate which metabolizes into salicylic acid, also known as asprin. They can also be used as a tea.

Wintergreen has been used as a poultice to stop bleeding, and to treat dog bites, snakebites, insect bites and other sores and wounds. It is an analgesic, diuretic, antiseptic, anti-spasmodic and anti-rheumatic.

Witch Hazel, *Hamamelis Virginiana*

Identification. Witch hazels, also known as winterbloom, are deciduous shrubs growing to 40 feet tall, with most under 25 feet tall. Alternating oval leaves are 2 to 6 inches long and 1 to 4 inches across. The current years flowers bloom as the previous year's fruit matures.

Edibility. The plant is potentially toxic and should not be eaten.

As a Remedy. The leaves and bark are used to produce the astringent decoction used externally in herbal medicine and skin care products. It is commonly used as a herbal remedy to treat diaper rash, sores, bruises, psoriasis, eczema, poison ivy, bug bites, and burns. It is also used to reduce swelling, especially after childbirth.

A tea made from the leaves and bark has been used topically for hemorrhoids and ulcers. It can also be used as a gargle for a sore throat and as a rinse for mouth sores.

Wood Sorrel, *Oxalis*

Identification. Wood sorrel is an annual or perennial that grows to be approximately 3 inches high.

The species is sometimes called false shamrocks for its arrangement of 3 heart-shaped leaves that are similar to clover. The white, pink, red or yellow flowers have 5 petals and 10 stamens.

Edibility. Wood sorrel is a commonly used food. The roots are starchy and taste similar to a potato when boiled. The leaves and stems are edible raw or cooked and can be chewed to alleviate thirst.

The lemony-tasting leaves can be dried to make a tasty tea. The leaves contain oxalic acid and should be cooked if they are eaten in large quantities or on a regular basis.

As a Remedy. Wood sorrel has been used as an aphrodisiac and as a treat for fever, cramps, nausea, mouth sores and sore throats. The leaves are high in vitamin C and can be used to prevent scurvy.

Yaupon, *Ilex Vomitoria*

Identification. Yaupon holly, also known as cassina, is an evergreen shrub commonly used as an ornamental plant in the southeastern United States.

The mature plant stands 16 to 30 feet tall, with smooth, gray bark and thin, hairy shoots. Alternate leaves are dark green and glossy on top and lighter in color on the underside. The fruit are small red or yellow berries containing 4 pits each.

Edibility. The leaves are used to brew a black tea that contains caffeine and theobromine. It can be used as an acceptable coffee substitute. The fruit is poisonous.

As a Remedy. A thick decoction of the leaves induces vomiting.

Yellow Birch, *Betula Alleghaniensis*

Identification. It is also known as golden birch. Identifiable by its golden-bronze exfoliating bark and the wintergreen scent of a scraped twig, the yellow birch is a valuable survival plant of the eastern United States.

Edibility. The inner bark, sap, young twigs, and leaves are all edible.

The inner bark can be eaten cooked. Dried and ground into a powder, it can be substituted for some of the flour in baked goods. Tea can be made by steeping the twigs and inner bark. Harvest the sap in early spring to use as a drink, concentrate it into a syrup, or ferment it into a beer.

As a Remedy. The plant is rarely used as a medicinal, although a decoction of the bark has been used as a blood purifier.

Yellow Rocket, *Barbarea*

Identification. Yellow rocket, also known as winter cress, American cress, Belle Isle cress and Scurvy cress, grows along rivers, streams, creeks and other wet areas. It is a perennial, growing up to 1 foot in height.

Edibility. Harvest the leaves when young and eat them raw or lightly cooked. Older leaves can be eaten, but they are strongly bitter. Cook them in several changes of water to reduce the bitterness. Unopened flower heads can be steamed like broccoli.

As a Remedy. The leaves of yellow rocket are used to make a poultice for treating wounds. Use the leaves to make a tea with diuretic properties.

TRAPPING IN WINTER FOR BEAVER AND MUSKRAT JUST LIKE OUR FOREFATHERS DID

- By S. Patrick –

"Feel what it's like to truly starve, and I guarantee that you'll forever think twice before wasting food."

– Criss Jami

I was born in Seattle, Washington, and since there's not much in the way of trapping going on up there, I was relocated at an early age to Lovell, Wyoming.

That's not actually the reason my family moved, but once I developed my passion for trapping, it was good enough for me.

In case you've never heard of Lovell, don't feel bad. Until I was relocated there at the age of eight, neither had I. In fact, I would guess that most folks couldn't point to it on a map without searching the whole state first.

Lovell is about 100 miles due east of what we call the park, which is Yellowstone National Park. I don't think Lovell has any bigger population now than when I was a kid 40 odd years ago; it's just stayed around 2,200 people.

The reason this area is so good for trapping is that it's right at the foothills of the Big Horn Mountains. It's the prime area for many miles around for hunting, fishing, and trapping.

So like many young boys back then in a small town with those types of opportunities, I trapped all winter and cut firewood and sold it or bucked hay and alfalfa all summer. I have to tell you that I greatly preferred trapping to bucking for reasons you may well imagine. Wyoming can get a little warm in the summer, and if you've ever bucked wet, heavy alfalfa in the sun, I don't have to tell you anymore.

Why Our Forefathers Trapped

Personally, I was trapping for the money. Growing up in a small town, it was a good way to make money during the winter months when things really slowed down in the summer job areas. Our forefathers, on the other hand, trapped for a variety of reasons, some of which may surprise you.

Yes, of course, there was the fur trade, so they obviously trapped for the money. As a matter of fact, many men who went bust in various gold or land rushes went on to make their fortunes in the fur trade.

One such man was John Jacob Astor. A German-born immigrant, he got his big break in the fur trade and went on to become a multimillionaire, a vast New York real estate owner, and a legendary patron of the arts.

The majority of our forefathers trapped for the money. However, many who traded in furs also used them as clothing for themselves and their families. They would quite typically feed the carcasses to their dogs, and a normal homestead had several. They would also use small, chopped pieces of the carcasses to drop in the seed hole along with their corn plantings. The pieces would decompose and provide nutrients for the corn stalks.

What we have to realize is that our forefathers trapped, hunted, farmed, and fished to stay alive. In most cases, they used every part of the animal or plant in ways that we have all but lost today. As an example, they would use the corn silk that we throw away today for at least five different natural remedies, including kidney stones and edema.

In truth, I wish we would go back to a lot of that and get away from all these drugs that are being pushed today.

The Best Places to Trap for Beaver and Muskrat

Beaver and muskrats' habitats range from Florida to Canada with the real exceptions being any of the arid states, such as Arizona, New Mexico, and others.

There have been a few dens found along the U.S. border with Mexico but definitely not in any appreciable quantities.

Most beavers weigh between 26 and 90 pounds with only a few making it to the 100-pound mark, according to fishwildlife.org. Muskrats usually weigh 1.3 to 4.4 pounds but are typically much more abundant, says fishwildlife.org.

Personally, the biggest beaver I ever trapped weighed in unofficially at 98 pounds. People came from all over town to see the monster. I got a lot of use out of the scale that day because, of course, they wanted to see the weight themselves.

The thing is, his pelt wasn't that good. He was old, and so the pelt was only given a grade B at the trading post.

Their Local Habitats

Beavers rely on freshwater areas for their habitats and mainly prefer areas with running water; I've yet to find any in stagnant waters at all. They like to follow trails, and that's a good thing for a trapper. Once you find a good trail, all that's typically needed is setting a good trap. We will discuss how to find their trails a little later.

Muskrats will inhabit many more types of wetland areas than you'll typically find beavers in. They will live in most any wetlands with an abundant supply of aquatic vegetation, such as swamps, coastal and freshwater marshes, lakes, ponds, and slow-moving streams. For the most part, they feed on aquatic plants, including cattails, duckweeds, water lilies, arrowheads, and sedges.

That really turns out to be your key with trapping muskrat. If you don't see anything they would consider food, then you're not likely to find any muskrats there.

Beaver, as you may know, eat mostly tree bark in the winter months in their huts or dens. Their preference is for aspen trees, but they will feed on almost any trees that have a good cambium layer to their bark.

Cambium is the soft, smooth inner layer of the bark, and beavers love it (and it's also edible for humans). However, during the summer months, they will feed on both bark and select aquatic plants.

The reason it's important to know what each of these critters feed on is that it will make you a much better trapper. Think about it…if you didn't know what they eat, you'd be at a disadvantage scouting places where you could be successful trapping them.

The Types of Traps You'll Use for Beaver and Muskrat

There are two main types of traps that you'll use when trapping for either beaver or muskrat: foot hold and body grip traps.

The foot hold trap is normally used along land-based trails that lead to the water. Body grip traps are most often used for underwater trails, which we will discuss later.

The foot hold traps don't need any teeth because the animal being trapped is so small that any teeth may just sever the leg instead of trapping the animal. The body grip traps don't have teeth either, because they grip a large part of the body and would put lots of holes in the pelt.

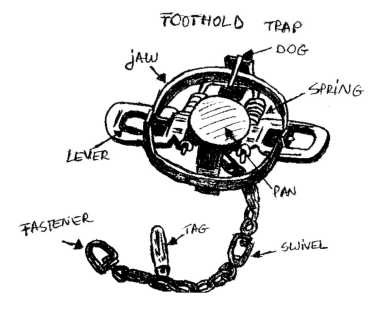

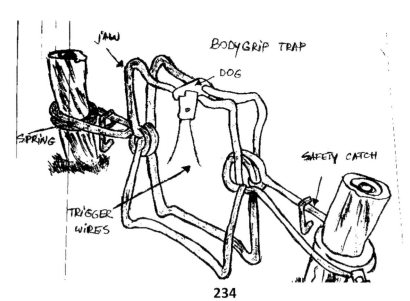

234

There are several other types of traps, such as snare—which may be illegal in many states—box traps, and more. The biggest reason box traps never took off in popularity is that it was pretty tough to put 100 of them on a mule and go set your trap line, whereas getting that many foot hold or body grip traps on your pack animal would be doable.

Later we'll discuss the methods I used to deploy each type of trap for best results. Having a selection of both is a really good idea since in one pond or creek area, you might well find you need both to effectively trap just that one area.

Foot Hold Trap Types

First off, you really have to talk about the two main trap types, which are long spring and coil spring traps. Long springs will come in singles or doubles.

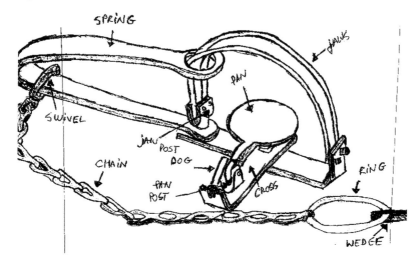

What that means is that they will have one long spring only on one side that snaps the trap shut. Or the doubles have two long springs, one to each side. If you're going after beaver and using long springs, I would suggest the double so that there isn't any doubt that the trap will close well and won't have any play in it where the beaver can get free.

Coil spring traps are much the same and can be had with one or two coils. Their coils are nearly always located on either side of the trigger, which could be a round or rectangle pan, as it's called. For the same reasons, I'm going to recommend double coils on your traps.

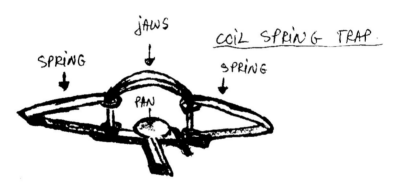

There are other big reasons why I always go with doubles:

1. Traps freeze shut. I've seen traps freeze shut after freezing rains that turned to ice and snow thaws that refroze. When your trap freezes up, you don't get your beaver or muskrat, plain and simple.

2. Debris falls onto your trap from the trees above or is blown there by the wind. Either way, you need a trap that will snap through all that mess and catch your critter.

3. The animal, especially a beaver with his weight of up to 100 pounds, can't sit on your long spring and have it open enough to get free if it's a single spring trap.

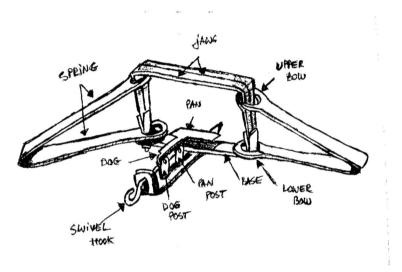

The Differences Between Long Spring and Coil Spring Traps

One of the really big differences is size.

Your average small game (beaver, fox, muskrat, and coyote) coil spring trap is only going to have an outside jaw spread of about 6 inches and a total footprint size of maybe 8 1/2 or 9 inches, depending mostly on the brand.

On the other hand, your long spring traps will have that same outside jaw area of only about 6 inches on average, but the springs themselves can be 8 to 12 inches each, and they stick out on either side. This can be problematic if you're setting your trap in a narrow trail or in between two trees or two rocks because the trail goes there. From my experience, both traps close equally as well and stay shut as well as the other, but the coil spring gives you a smaller trap that can fit into tight spots.

The thing about coil spring traps to be wary of is that the spring levers can be treacherous to keep your boots on so they don't slip if the conditions are muddy and mucky. Most trappers will step on both sides at the same time when they are lowering the jaws to set the trap. Slipping with your fingers in there can be painful at best. Just be mindful of that, and I'm sure you'll do great.

The long spring traps give you a spring to step on that's up to a foot long on both sides. The coil spring can be only an inch per side at the top before you get it flattened out. Slipping at that moment is not advised. Lots of trappers have fouled up hands from just such occurrences.

Finding the Land Trails

The things you really want to look for are food scrap piles, tree gnawing marks, trail starts at any water's edge, and droppings. Food scrap piles can be found for both beaver and muskrat. The beaver likes the inside, soft, tasty portion of the trees' bark, or they will eat all the new, soft bark offshoots and soft branch twig ends. If food is plentiful, you'll find that they will leave piles of bark with just the soft inner layer scraped out.

Muskrat and beaver will chew off a larger part of a plant and then only eat the choicest parts if there is a good food supply. When they do this, they leave a food scrap pile that is easy to see.

If you see tree gnawing signs about 4 to 10 inches off the ground where it looks like it was done by a small chisel that took out small gouges, then you quite likely have a beaver in the area.

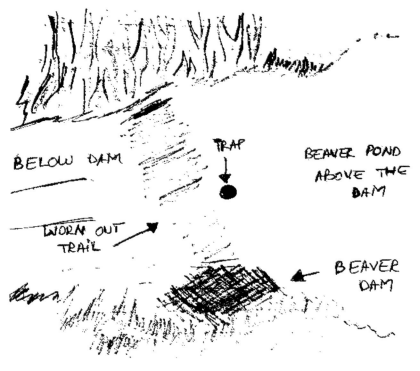

BELOW DAM

TRAP

BEAVER POND ABOVE THE DAM

WORN OUT TRAIL

BEAVER DAM

Both beaver and muskrat never get far from the water, so walk the water's edge and find a spot where the grass is pushed down or earth is exposed really close to the water. It may even appear to be a tunnel in the grass as the grass has grown around it.

That's where you're going to want to set your foot hold trap or, depending on the situation, maybe a body grip trap; we'll get into how to decide that later.

How to Set the Foot Hold Trap

One of the mistakes people make is wanting to cover their traps with brush or other camouflage, but beavers and muskrats don't know what a trap looks like and have no real natural fear of it.

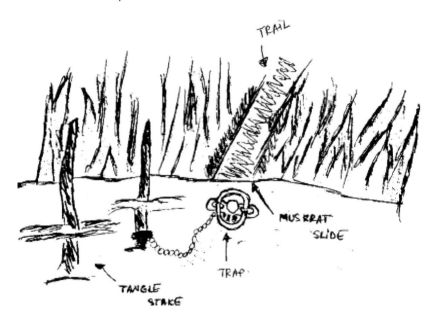

However, the brush you put on top of your trap can cause it to not close fully or properly, and you will miss your critter. Then they might learn not to like that strange metal thingy.

Be sure to stake down your trap really well or wire it to a tree. If not, when you come back and find it gone, you know you have a critter swimming somewhere with your trap on it. Just set your trap in the middle so they can't avoid it, and you should be good.

Finding the Underwater Trails

If you have a beaver hut or lodge and you have clear ice with no snow on top, then look for a trail of bubbles leading to the hut. If you have snow on the ice, be sure to clear it away so you can find the bubble trail.

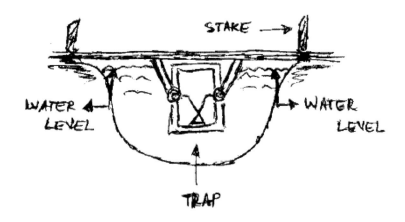

How to Set a Body Grip Trap

Once you find the bubble trail, take an ax and cut a square hole out of the ice. Then pull out your ice chunks. Use a body grip trap, and put a peeled potato on the trigger prongs. Be sure to check with your local laws to ensure baiting traps are legal in your area.

Put the trap on its setting stick (this is just a good stick you found) then chain it to its cross stick that stays on top of the ice to keep the trap there. That stick needs to be longer than the hole is wide, or the critter will get away with your trap. When you come back, you'll likely have a beaver in that trap.

If you can't find a bubble trail, look for narrow spots in the creek, and set the traps there. If there are none, you can bet that the entrance to the hut will be pretty much facing the water. Just set the body grip trap 10 feet from the hut to the center of it in the same way by chopping a hole in the ice, etc.

Tanning

There are a ton of manuals out there on skinning, so I won't go into that, but I will give some tips on tanning.

First off, never pull your hide tight and let your dogs de-fat the hide for you. I know a lot of people do that, but it's a mistake. Here's why. Your dogs don't know when you have added your tanning mixture to the hide. Alum is aluminum sulfate, which is not good for dogs, and the soda will give them gas so bad you'll wish you hadn't done that if it's an indoor dog.

Once you're ready, mix up this little recipe.

- ❖ 2/3 cup Arm and Hammer Super Washing Soda
- ❖ 1 cup non-iodized salt
- ❖ 2 ½ cups alum

This mix is enough for one good-sized beaver, six to eight muskrats, or four to five good-sized rabbits. You can de-fat either before or after you soak your hides for the first soak; you may find it easier to do afterwards.

Fill a five-gallon bucket with about three gallons of warm, but not hot, water. Add the salt, and mix with a wooden stick until the salt is dissolved. Then add the aluminum sulfate and the washing soda. Stir again until the chemicals are dissolved. It will be a little effervescent, but that's okay.

Drop the hide(s) in the bucket, and gently stir with a stick. You can use a non-metallic weight to hold the hide under water if it tries to float. Make sure your weights are non-metallic or you'll have a worthless hide in no time with green spots on it. Only use a wooden stick and a rope-type clothesline (you'll understand the clothesline later) for the same reason.

Stir, lift out, and re-immerse your hides once a day for three days. If you have not defatted your hide yet, do so after the three-day mark. Then look at your solution. If it's fatty, dirty, and oily, as it will be most of the time, then make a fresh batch using the same recipe.

Then soak your hides for four to 11 more days, depending on the thickness and feel of the hide. Rabbit will usually tan well after seven days, whereas beaver is usually 14 days.

Now wring out your hide by hand really well and hang over a clothesline indoors overnight with the flesh side down and the fur side up. You want to dry the fur but not the hide. The reason for doing this indoors is that dogs and critters will come take your prize right off the line if it's outdoors.

Now you need to start breaking your hide. Each day, knead it together like bread. Rotate it in a circle, and knead it from every direction. This is how you end up with a nice, soft hide instead of something that feels like a board. When the hide is fully dry and not cool to the touch, then you are finished with that hide.

Selling at the Trading Post

The trader is going to do his best to buy your furs cheap. That's his job, so don't take offense at it. Your beaver will have reached his fur peak between December and March, so if you trapped during those times, you'll have a good shot at a decent-priced pelt.

Blow on the fur in one direction, and you'll see that there is what's called under-fur. To be a prime fur, this should be between 0.8"–1.2" long in the kidney area of the beaver. The guard hairs (the longer outer hairs) should be between 2"–2.4" long.

Then, of course, you'll have all the normal sundries of him saying, "Well, the hide's nicked here," or "The split line on your skinning was off, so it's not symmetrical," or other such things so he can barter you down. Like I said, this is normal, and your job is to refute his claims of course.

And There You Have It

Now you can trap for beaver and muskrat just like our forefathers did. These are much the same methods they used with the exception that a small number of trappers used brain tanning methods. Most of those furs could not be sold to the European markets because the smell was considered unsavory, so the practice of brain tanning died out.

Follow all the above and you'll be a successful trapper in no time.

DEER HUNTING BASICS AND STEPS TO HIDE TANNING

- By Hunter Riley -

"We will see the day when we live on what we produce. "

— Marion G. Romney

Deer hunting is as old as civilization and provided our ancestors with a source of lean protein as well as material for clothing and shelter. The last 100 years has seen a shift away from hunting deer out of necessity into one of sport and keeping our hunting skills sharp, a tribute to those ancient humans.

It's a stretch even to attempt to cover how to hunt deer in such a small amount of space, but we are going to lay out the basics of deer hunting for those looking to begin a lifelong pursuit.

As we will discuss, the practice of utilizing everything a deer has to offer has seen a renaissance in the hunting world, a trend we hope continues.

Everyone knows what to do with the meat, but an often-underutilized part of the deer is the hide. In this chapter, we will also take a look at the steps to correctly tan a whole deer hide.

245

Deer Hunting Basics

We're going to go into this with the assumption that you understand the basic gear involved with deer hunting. You know, the gun or bow and camo.

What we want to outline in this first section are the basics of locating deer, understanding their behavior, and how you go about finding and setting up for a harvest.

What Deer Need

Having a basic understanding of what deer need to survive allows you to make your initial scouting much more efficient.

So, what do deer need to survive? Water is of course, essential for all living creatures on Earth, deer included. Deer normally do not have large home ranges and generally will stay around a five mile or less radius. If you can find a water source such as a pond or creek, there is going to be a deer population in the area.

One of the first steps to scouting an area and determining where deer traffic is found is to determine food sources in the area. If there are crops in the area, you can bet that there will be deer feeding in those areas consistently early in the season and up to rut.

Deer also feed heavily on browse, such as woody plants, as well as mast (nuts and fruits). All of these foods are going to attract deer and during the early and late season, should be your focus point and branching out from there to find deer.

Deer also need a form of shelter. This often in the form of heavier brush or thickets where they can escape from predators. These areas are also places deer like to bed down. You will often find deer holding, especially in the colder winter months, on the southeast side of embankments or land rises which protect them from brutal winds.

If you can nail down these three requirements from scouting and maps, you can be confident that you will be in an area that is patrolled by deer.

When Deer Move

Understanding when deer are the most active allow you to be in the woods during these times. For just about any time during the year, especially during the season, deer are usually going to be more active at night making the best times to hunt them early in the morning, when they are moving back to bed, and late in the afternoon when they are moving to begin eating.

This is not always the case as there have been thousands of deer taken in the middle of the day. Regarding activity though, early daylight hours and the last two hours of shooting light have the highest deer activities.

Things can change during the peak of the deer mating season, the rut, where deer are moving just about at all hours of the day.

The most important aspect is not only understanding when deer are moving but their routes. Deer are creature of habit and will often hold to the same travel lanes if not disturbed.

Scouting before the season and looking for tracks and scat in areas where there is a noticeable path through the woods or vegetation will give you a decent idea of these travel lanes and can be extrapolated to feeding and bedding areas.

Deer Behavior in Different Seasons

Though this is a generalization, for this chapter we can split the normal deer season into three distinct time periods based on how deer are behaving.

Early Season:

During the early season deer are focused on feeding, and they are feeding hard. With scouting and observing deer movements, you can pin down times and locations of deer movement. Though it's much easier said than done, the early season is the easiest period for predicting when and where the deer are going to be at.

Rut:

We could write a book, and there are several out there, on deer behavior during the rut. Rut often occurs around the first real cold snap and usually ranges around mid-November in most areas. During this time, bucks are searching hard for does and breeding takes the place of feeding. It's much more difficult to predict deer movements during this time. If you have located rubs and know areas where deer are localizing, you can use estrous scents and even rattling to increase your chances of success. There will also be periods during the rut where deer activity seems to fall off dramatically. This is because a lot of bucks are bedded down with does and can last for several days. Activity usually picks up back to rut levels shortly after.

Late Season:

After the rut has concluded, usually after two to three weeks, the focus switches back to feeding. Deer are in their worst state of the year at this point and are in high need of food after spending the last month breeding. If there are winter crops in the area, these will be magnets for deer.

Browse is most often the top food source in non-agricultural hunting grounds as well as any leftover mast from earlier in the fall.

How to Set Up

There are several strategies for getting the drop on deer. If you have done your homework and have an idea of the general area deer are in, and their travel lanes, the most common method is an ambush. Setting up a tree stand or blind along these areas with clear shooting lanes and sitting and waiting for the deer to show up.

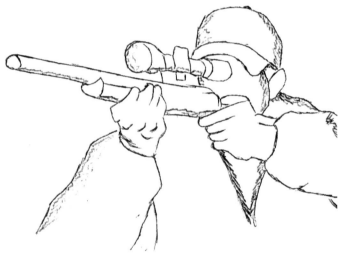

How close you are to travel lanes or feeding areas is going to depend on your choice of weapon as well. With a rifle or muzzleloader, there is no reason to be set up in dense growth right over or on a trail where your chances for spooking deer is much greater. All situations are different, and part of becoming an efficient deer hunter is putting yourself in those positions and having success and failures and learning how to adapt to what is around you and how the deer are behaving.

Scoping or glassing deer from a distance and then positioning yourself for a shot is another popular method and demands more physical fitness and another level of strategy. This method is great when hunting more open areas that contain changes in elevation where you can view large areas of land. In dense woods, this tactic is much more difficult.

Regardless of the tactics that you choose to go with, there is a level of woodsmanship that goes along with success. You need to keep your sound and scent footprint down to minimum. Being quiet in the woods just comes with practice, but you can always be cautious with your scent.

Using a scent masker is a good start, but more than anything you need to have yourself positioned downwind of where you expect deer to be. You can have all the equipment, done all the scouting, and have a fantastic setup, but if you have not accounted for the wind direction and yours and the deer's location, it will all be in vain.

After the Harvest/The Hide

At the advent of hunting, taking a deer was not just a sport but a means of survival.

Too often hunters simply take the animals for the antler rack and neglect such valuable parts of the deer.

We have seen a trend back towards the full utilization of the deer, and we believe it is for the best.

Even with this trend of taking advantage of all of the resources a harvested deer can provide, the hide is still shamefully neglected. Most often the deer hide is used for decorations purposes, but the hide and buckskin can also be used to make wonderfully soft and beautiful garments and pouches if you have or know someone with the requisite skill set. Tanning your hide is also going to save you a good deal of money compared to farming out the process to others.

Tanning Guide: Step by Step

Removing the Hide:
We are going to focus more on the tanning process than the removal, but generally, we like to work with a hide that has been removed from above the tarsal glands on the back legs to below the jaw.

This gives a full hide that can be used for a variety of clothing or decoration purposes.

All cuts should be made on the inside of the body as this will make a better-looking hide in our opinion. You will also need to debone the tail if you want that part of the hide included.

Removing the Flesh:

Once the hide is removed, you will notice that the underside of the hide still has a layer of cartilage and other tissue. Removing all of this is critical to having a well-preserved hide and makes the tanning process much more effective. We don't like using a sharp knife; it is too easy to cut through or damage the hide.

A duller knife that still has a slight edge is the best tool to use. This process is extensive and time-consuming, but it has to be done to have an evenly tanned hide. You will notice a white layer of skin, and this is right below the hairline. Be sure to not cut through this layer.

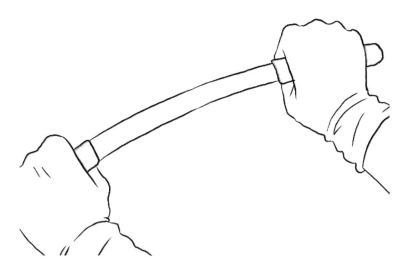

Hair or No Hair:

From here you have two options for the hide. You can keep the hair on or remove the hair to make buckskin. If you want to move forward with the hair intact jump ahead to step 5. To remove the hair from the hide and make a buckskin, mix 1 gallon of hardwood ashes, 2 pounds of household lime (slaked), and 5 gallons of warm water. Stir the mixture until everything is dissolved.

Completely immerse the deerskin in the mixture. Stir the mixture several times a day until the hair comes off easily. This will take at least 2 to 3 days and maybe a fourth. Be sure to check every day, keeping the skin in this solution for too long will cause it to deteriorate.

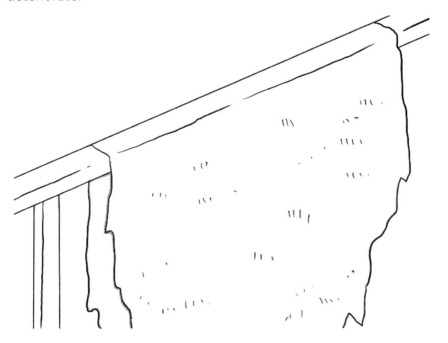

Removing the Hair:

Place the hide on a raised surface with the hair side up. Use the back of a knife to scrape off the hair and then rinse the skin several times with clean water.

You then need to soak the hide for 24 hours in a mixture of 5:1 ratio of water to vinegar. Stir this mixture with the hide in it every few hours.

Once the skin has soaked for 24 hours, soak the hide in the clean water overnight. This step neutralizes and removes the lime and ash mixture and keeps the hide from deteriorating.

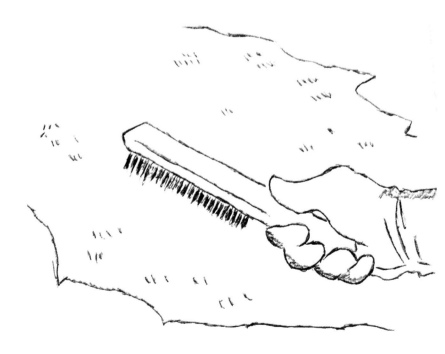

Salting:

Once you have the flesh removed and/or removed the hair it's time to salt the hide hard. You can't over salt the hide, so be sure to be generous with it. We like non-iodized salt because it will not cause the hide to stain. What the salt is doing it drying out the moisture from the hide. Several pounds of salt should be used. Work it into the hide and let the hide sit overnight. From here you can continue with the tanning process or freeze the hide for later work. Salting also helps loosen up any leftover pieces of tissue so be sure to go through one more round of scraping before moving on.

Cleaning the Hide:

Before we get into the actual process of tanning, you need to wash as much of the salt off the hide as possible. We like to soak the hide in several gallons of clean water for several hours and then going over the skin side of the hide with the backside of a knife or a similar surface. Having absorbent towels to blot dry is also very effective.

Tanning:

There are some options you have for tanning the hide. There are commercial tanning solutions that are probably the most convenient. Another option is a salt/aluminum alum solution. The commercial kits often come with directions and usually take 4-5 days of soaking the hide or just rubbing in the solution and letting it sit for several days.

We soak our hides in large trashcans or buckets that will be able to hold at least 8 gallons of water easily. The most common homemade tanning solution is made from 2.5lbs of salt in 4gallons of water with 1lb of ammonia alum that has been added to 1 gallon of water and is slowly added to the salt solution. The hide should be stirred several times every day. Some tanners will tell you to refrigerate the soaking hide, but as long as the weather outside is staying under 45°F, it should be fine outdoors as long as it is covered.

Draining the Hide:

This step is especially important if you have to soak the hide for several days rather than let the hide sit with a tanning solution rubbed into it. When using a soaking method, take out the hide and rinse it gently with water and allow it to drain for an hour. You do not want it to dry out completely as it is much more difficult to soften the hide in this state. Once you have a moist hide that is not dripping, we like to add some oil or fat liquor into the hide.

Softening the Hide:

At the end of the tanning process, however, you went about tanning and drying, you're going to have a stiff hide. Our favorite way to work the stiffness out is to use a saw horse, but any line or piece of flat surface you can pull the hide over will work. As you stretch the hide and work it over the flat surface, you will begin to tell by feel the leather begin to loosen up and have a more subtle feel.

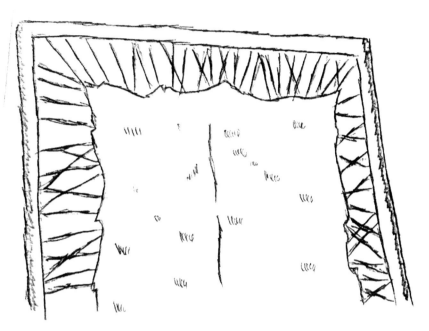

As the hide dries, moisten the skin lightly with a spray bottle of damp cloth and pull the hide back and forth over the sawhorse, dampening the hide as needed, until you have the hide as soft as you want it. During this process, you can also continue to add some oil or fat liquor as needed.

Conclusion

Hunting deer is a long process. It begins with scouting the land and studying deer movements, moves to getting boots in the field trying to harvest a deer, and hopefully ends with you utilizing as much of the deer as possible.

There is a plethora of information on deer hunting that is available. This is by no means an in-depth discussion on the intricacies of deer hunting, but we hope that it outlines some of the basic ideas behind the sport and provides a proven and detailed guide on how to utilize on of the most underused part of the deer. You might find it time-consuming or you might find that it becomes part of the ritual of harvesting deer. Whatever it becomes, we hope you at least try it once.

HOW TO MAKE CHARCOAL

- By F. Mason -

"The future belongs to the few of us still willing to get our hands dirty."

— Roland Tiangco

For most of us charcoal is just something you pick up at the gas station when you plan to fire up the grill. If you're an artist you might also use sticks of it for sketching. Beyond that, it isn't something we usually have a lot of use for.

If you want to smelt iron, or most other metals, charcoal is an essential part of the process. It's one of the few easily obtained fuels that can produce the high temperatures required for a long enough time to extract metal from ore. It's the fuel you need to power a forge for blacksmithing. If civilization ever falls far enough that we need to rebuild basic metallurgy from scratch, we're going to need lots of charcoal.

It has other uses too. Charcoal is excellent at soaking up contaminants, so it's valuable if you plan to build a water filtration system. Powdered clean charcoal, taken orally, can help with some stomach upsets. Add sulfur and saltpeter to finely ground charcoal and you have black powder. It's useful stuff.

Unfortunately, a post-SHTF raid on your local Exxon might not supply the charcoal you need. A lot of modern charcoal is briquettes, and they're far from pure – they're made from powdered charcoal or carbonized sawdust, bound together with clay and lime. Even lumpwood charcoal often has chemical additives, to repel dampness or make it easier to light. If you want pure charcoal the chances are you're going to have to make it yourself.

Luckily this isn't exactly a high-tech process, but it *does* take a bit of knowledge and skill. Charcoal is simply wood that's been heated to a very high temperature, but starved of the oxygen it needs to burn. This process removes water and various organic substances, leaving a residue that's very high in carbon. Modern industrial charcoal production involves heating wood or sawdust (and sometimes other materials, like coconut shell) in an airtight steel container called a retort. It's possible to do this yourself, but heating it to a high enough temperature for hours (or even days) will use a *lot* of fuel. Mostly for this reason your best bet is to use a more traditional technique, which uses wood as both the fuel and feedstock.

Traditional charcoal burners in the UK made charcoal by lighting a wood fire then covering it with turf and soil. This mound was called a clamp, like the earth-covered vegetable stores we've talked about before. A charcoal clamp works by starting a burn that's hot enough to char the entire pile of wood, but sealing it so little or no oxygen can get in. Usually charcoal burners would build and cover the stack, leaving a small tunnel to a bundle of kindling at the center; then they'd push a burning torch into the tunnel, let the fire take hold, fill the tunnel with wood then seal off the outer end. A small hole at the top would be left to let smoke out, and when the color of the smoke changed from gray-green to blue – showing that the wood was dry- that would be covered too.

A commercial clamp could be huge – twenty to thirty feet in diameter, and containing tons of wood. A clamp that size would take weeks to burn and it had to be watched all the time; if the fire broke through the covering the hole had to be quickly plugged, or the entire pile would blaze up and be reduced to ash. The temperature inside a clamp is extremely high, and if oxygen manages to get in the whole thing will erupt into flames.

Luckily, it's possible to build and burn a much smaller clamp – anything from about ten pounds of wood and up will work fine. A smaller clamp means a shorter burn time, all the way down to three or four hours for a very small one that yields a couple of pounds of charcoal. The clamp in the photos used about 25 pounds of seasoned wood and produced just over six pounds of charcoal.

To build a clamp, first collect your wood. Don't underestimate how much you'll need here: Making charcoal with a clamp isn't the most efficient process. However much wood you put in, count on getting about half as much charcoal by volume and a fifth as much by weight. This is just the way the process works; some of the wood is used as fuel to char the rest. A bigger clamp will be more efficient, but you'll still be lucky to get two-thirds the volume you started with.

You also need to consider what *kind* of wood you want. Softwood is best avoided if possible. It will work, sort of, but the charcoal you end up with will burn quickly and generate less heat. Hardwood is much better. Apple and hickory are traditional favorites for grilling, but to be honest once it's been turned into charcoal any flavor from the wood is pretty much gone. What matters is to use hard, dense wood; it has more carbon in it, and will produce higher quality charcoal.

Clear a patch of level ground and, in the center of it, make a small platform of dry split sticks. On top of this build a mound of tinder – paper, dry leaves or anything else that will catch easily – then build a cone of split sticks around it. Leave a gap at one side so you can ignite it.

Now start to add larger sticks and logs. Prop these against the cone and build the stack outwards. Keep it packed as tightly as you can. With a normal fire you want small gaps to let air flow through the

fuel, but there isn't going to be any airflow inside your clamp. The charring process will pass from one log to the next by radiated heat and contact, so the closer the logs are, the better. Fill in any gaps with smaller sticks to keep the mass as solid as possible. The only exception is the tunnel you'll leave from the outside of the pile to the tinder in the middle.

Once the stack is fully built it needs to be covered. The first layer of covering should be turf. This prevents too much soil from mixing in with the charcoal during the process. The clamp in the photos was built in a damp wooded area, and chunks of moss were used for the first layer.

Then cover this with loose soil, leaving a chimney hole at the top and a space to light it through. If the soil is dry it should be damped down with water – not enough to soak it, just to keep it damp.

Now the clamp is ready to light. Depending on how big it is you might be able to roll up some paper, light the end and shove it into the tinder, or you might need to make a torch as long as your tunnel. However you do it, set fire to the tinder in the middle and let it catch properly. Wait until the small sticks are well on fire and the fuel is catching. It's better to err on the side of caution here; letting an extra one or two percent of the wood burn is a lot less hassle than closing it up too early, so it goes out and you have to open it up and start again.

When the fire has a good hold in the center of the clamp, fill the tunnel with wood and close off the outside with turf and soil. At this point there should be smoke coming from the chimney and, probably, quite a few other places on the outside of the clamp. Don't worry about the occasional wisp, but if any spots are smoking steadily block them with a handful of soil. Then let it cook for a little while.

If you've used dry, seasoned wood the chances are the smoke will already be clear and blue; if so you can close off the chimney after a few minutes. If the clamp is built of green wood there will be a lot more smoke, and it will be greenish-gray and acrid. Leave the chimney open until it turns blue, then seal it off with a piece of turf and a shovelful of earth.

Now you have to be patient – and observant. The clamp needs to be watched *constantly*, because if the covering breaks open and air gets in, all your charcoal will catch fire and burn in minutes. If smoke begins to appear in a new spot, throw some more soil on. If parts of the covering sag or show cracks, add more soil. If a flame appears smother it with a piece of turf right away, then reinforce

the spot with soil. Every so often sprinkle water over it, or give it a fine spray with a hose, to keep the soil damp.

Don't ever assume that because you've been watching your clamp for six hours and nothing has happened, it's safe to leave it for half an hour while you go and wash the smell of woodsmoke out of your hair. It isn't. If the covering breaks and air gets in, it's going to burn *fast*. And if it's a windy day, and a few hundred pounds of charcoal has lit off, it's going to be generating blast furnace temperatures. You won't even be able to get near it, never mind put it out.

There will always be a few tiny wisps of smoke appearing, but eventually these will stop. When that happens you'll know about it, because of course you've been constantly watching the clamp. If they've stopped that means the burn is done; there's no wood left to char. It's (finally) time to take the clamp apart.

Before you start to break it open get some buckets of water or, better, a hose. There's still going to be a lot of heat inside and it can flare up when the oxygen hits it, destroying all your work at the last minute. Be ready to put out any flames. Having a stack of wet chunks of turf ready is a good idea.

Now start to open up one side. Shift the outer layer of soil, then pull the turf away. More likely than not the first thing you'll see is unburned wood. Relax; this doesn't mean it hasn't worked. The covering usually pulls heat away from the outer layer of wood fast enough to prevent it charring. The larger the clamp, the smaller the percentage of unburned wood will be.

Clear away the remaining wood and you should see a mass of charcoal, which might still be glowing red. Use a shovel to start moving it out of the clamp and spreading it on a patch of clear ground or a fireproof surface – concrete is good. Then, if you have a hose, spray it with a fine mist of water to cool it down. Otherwise sprinkle water from your buckets over it. If you don't cool it down it can burn, but try to avoid soaking it. Progressively take the clamp to pieces, removing the cover from one section at a time and shoveling the charcoal out.

Finally you should have the entire clamp uncovered and dismantled, with your charcoal damped down and spread out on a fireproof surface. Now all you have to do is collect it, separate out any unburned wood and let it dry if you've accidentally soaked it.

Making charcoal isn't hard; it just needs attention to detail and a bit of time. Once you've mastered it you'll be able to make large amounts of an extremely useful substance. Charcoal is renewable – the raw material is simple wood – and being able to make it lets you create industrial essentials like a forge or blast furnace. If you're serious about being prepared for the worst a societal collapse could throw at you, this is an essential skill to have.

HOW TO MAKE ACTIVATED CHARCOAL

- By F. Mason -

"Any task completed with a clean conscience and dirty hands is one well earned. And to be proud of."

– *Chris Lumpkin*

Charcoal has many uses, and not long ago we looked at how valuable it can be in a SHTF scenario. Forget grilling your steaks; a reliable supply of it will let you build and run a forge or even a blast furnace. No matter how far society has fallen, being able to make charcoal gives you the foundation to start rebuilding metal-working industries.

Don't just think of charcoal as a fuel, though – it has a lot more uses than that. With a bit of preparation it's a great material for purifying chemicals, filtering water, even treating poisoning. What kind of preparation? Basically you need to turn it from normal charcoal into *activated* charcoal. This article will tell you how to do that.

What Is Activation?

Charcoal is mostly carbon. It's made from wood or other organic material that's been heated enough to burn out most of the chemicals in it, leaving the carbon behind. This makes it very useful, because carbon reacts with a lot of chemicals. If you run dirty water through a carbon filter all the large particles will be filtered out – and the dissolved chemicals will react with the carbon, and be removed that way.

The problem is only the surface of the carbon reacts, so once the atoms on the surface have been used up it loses its effects. One way to solve this is by increasing the surface area, so more atoms are available to react – and the best way to increase the surface area is to make the charcoal porous, so it's filled will millions of tiny holes.

Take an ounce of regular charcoal, with no cracks in it. This would make a cube about an inch on a side, and its surface area would be about six square inches. Turn that into activated charcoal powder and you have the same volume, but its surface area is now almost 900,000 square feet – more than *20 acres*. By activating charcoal you increase its chemical power by a stunning amount.

Making It At Home

So you've decided that activated charcoal is useful stuff to have around; now where do you get it? You can buy it, but that isn't an option after the SHTF, so it's best to make it yourself. Luckily that isn't hard. You already know how to make charcoal, so you have a unlimited supply of your main raw material. Now you just need a basic chemical and you can make all the activated charcoal you need.

The chemical you're looking for is calcium chloride. It's easily available and not expensive; you can get a 25 pound sack of it on ebay for less than $15. The best idea is to spend a bit more and get food grade crystals; that will cost you about $100 for a 50 pound sack. You won't need that much for making activated charcoal, but it has plenty other uses. It's better than salt for deicing roads. A solution of it sprayed on dirt tracks will keep dust down and prevent erosion. Adding some to canned vegetables will help keep them firm, or add salty flavor to pickles. It can help replace electrolytes if you're sweating a lot or have diarrhea. You can even use it to make self-heating meals, like the flameless heaters the

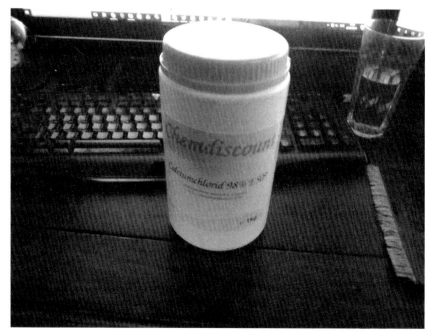

military issue with MREs - one of its most obvious features is that when you dissolve it in water it gives off quite a lot of heat.

To make activated charcoal, start out by picking through a batch of home-made charcoal. Look for pieces that are clean and fully charred – no ash or unburned wood.

Break the charcoal up as small as you can. You can start by double-bagging it in strong paper sacks, or putting it between two sheets of baking paper, and using a rolling pin to crush it.

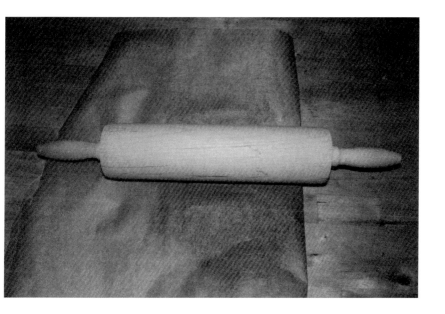

Next, mix the charcoal with an equal amount of calcium chloride by weight and grind the mixture to a powder. Use a mortar and pestle to grind it fine; for small amounts a coffee grinder will also work. The important thing 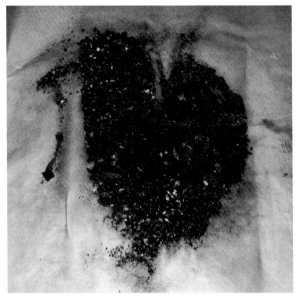 here is that it has to be as fine as you can get it, and thoroughly mixed. If there are a few small chips of calcium chloride that won't matter much, but what you really want is a uniform, fine gray powder.

Put the mixture in a glass or steel bowl. Don't use a plastic or aluminum one, because they might react chemically as you're working. Your main priority right through the process is to avoid any chemical contamination, because that will use up some of the charcoal's absorbent capabilities before you've even finished making it.

Now add water to the powder. Don't use water straight out of the faucet, because that will have chemicals in it. Purified or distilled water will work fine; otherwise run tap water through a carbon filter. You need to add three times as much water by weight as there is calcium chloride, so if you used four ounces of crystals add twelve ounces *by weight* of water. Quickly, but thoroughly, mix the water into the powder. Watch out; the mixture will heat up quickly as soon as you mix water with it, and can cause burns.

Some people will tell you that you can mix a solution of calcium chloride then add it to the powdered charcoal. This is wrong; unless you can mix them at a temperature of about 1,400°F all you'll get is wet charcoal. You need to grind the charcoal and calcium chloride together while they're dry. Once water is added the solution will quickly heat up, and because they've been ground together (not just mixed) every particle of charcoal will have calcium chloride sticking to its surface. When it's wetted and heated up this stresses the charcoal, opening microscopic cracks and pores all over its surface – activating it.

Now you need to leave it to dry. The quickest way to do this is to get tightly woven cotton – an old bedsheet will do – and cover a large steel or glass bowl with it. First, wash the cotton in plain water to get rid of any detergents or laundry conditioner then let it dry.

Top tip – don't use your best shirt for this, because it's going to be pretty difficult to shift the black stain from it when you're done.

Now pour the charcoal mix on top of the cotton. Rinse it with more pure water to flush out any calcium chlorate that's left in it, and leave it overnight or longer if necessary.

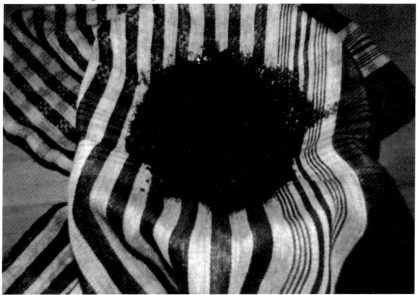

Collect the water that's dripped into the bowl – it's going to be pretty black, because there will be tiny particles of activated charcoal in it. This will also be the finest, and best, charcoal – so collect it by straining through a coffee filter.

When all the water has drained through turn the filter inside out and scrape off the charcoal. You won't get a lot, but this is *very* high grade; you might want to store it separately and keep it for internal use.

If you need your charcoal in a hurry you can filter the water out with the cotton, collect the fine particles with the coffee filter, then spread it all on a cookie sheet and bake it dry in the oven – the hotter the better. Just make sure the cookie sheet is completely clean before you start, and doesn't have any traces of dish soap on it.

Once the charcoal has completely dried, store it in an airtight jar and shake it well. It tends to cake itself into small lumps as it dries, but shaking will turn it back into powder.

What's it for?

Activated charcoal's superpower is in absorbing chemicals. It's particularly good at collecting poisons and toxins, from almost anywhere. If you need a water filter you can easily make one using activated charcoal as the filter element. Tightly pack a small, finely woven cloth bag with it, jam it into the end of a pipe and you have an effective filter; water flowing through the pipe will be clean and pure when it comes out the other end.

If someone has swallowed poison, get them to chase it with activated charcoal – an ounce for children, two to four ounces for an adult. Bleach, aspirin, acetaminophen, opiates and many other common poisons will be rapidly absorbed by the charcoal as soon as it reaches the stomach, and that prevents it getting into the bloodstream. It's also effective for many cases of mild food poisoning – bacteria, and the toxins they produce, get trapped in it too.

A paste of activated charcoal and any natural oil – coconut or olive are best – makes a good salve for insect bites or stings. The oil keeps it in place, and the charcoal draws the poison out of the bite. The oil's large molecules aren't easily trapped in the charcoal, so there won't be much effect on its absorbent powers.

If you tend to get gas after a meal, here's some good news: activated charcoal can reduce the symptoms. Just take half a teaspoon after eating and wash it down with a big glass of water. I can't promise that will completely eliminate the problem, but it will certainly help!

HOW TO MAKE A GAS MASK WITH ACTIVATED CHARCOAL

- By F. Mason -

"Skill is the unified force of experience, intellect and passion in their operation."

– John Ruskin

In World War I, poison gas attacks took the Allies in the trenches on the Western Front by surprise. After a few unsuccessful attempts to find protection against chemical attacks, the British found a dead German soldier with his gasmask on and replicated the model. By January 1917 the British and US Army made the standard issue gas which is very similar with the one in use today: both use activated charcoal.

The sarin attack in Syria showed just how dangerous chemical weapons can be. That was a clumsy attack, possibly even an accidental release of sarin from a rebel weapons dump, but it still managed to kill more than eighty people and injure hundreds more. A major attack carried out by a competent military could be nearly as destructive as a nuclear strike.

It's not only chemical weapons you have to worry about, either. What about a major industrial accident? In December 1984, the safety systems on a storage tank at a pesticide factory in Bhopal,

India, failed; the tank over pressurized and burst, releasing 32 tons of toxic gases. By next morning close to 4,000 people were dead. An EMP attack would cause hundreds of toxic chemical leaks all over the USA as safety systems were knocked out; potentially, millions could die.

When a chemical cloud drifts over you there's nowhere to hide, unless you happen to have a fully sealed military-grade shelter. The only thing that's going to save you is a gas mask. Your emergency equipment should include a properly fitted gas mask, and at least three in-date filter canisters, for every person in your home. Unfortunately, this can be expensive. You'll find plenty of ex-military gas masks on eBay, but most of them are obsolete foreign ones – and where are you going to find canisters for a Soviet or Israeli gas mask?

Even when canisters do appear they're usually old ones, and most likely they're totally ineffective. You can only rely on a canister if it's still sealed inside its foil pack and inside the expiration date printed on the foil. If you can find a reasonably modern NATO gas mask you might have more luck; these all use canisters with a standard 40mm thread, and there are a few companies that sell military spec ones.

If you can't get gas masks, and there's a chemical threat, you're going to have to make one. There are easy ways to do that. If you can get your hands on a full-face industrial anti-dust mask that's already a good start. These are commonly used by people who spray-paint or work with power tools, and they're good at blocking particles. They won't protect you from poisonous gases, but with some activated charcoal you can fix that easily enough.

Carefully open the canister. With some models, you can just lever the front plate off; others, you'll have to cut them open. Inside you'll find layers of fiber filter material. Take out all but the last layer and stand the canister flat on its base. Now cover the last layer of fiber with about a quarter of an inch of activated charcoal. Make sure it's evenly spread out and completely covers the fiber. Now put the other layers back until the canister is full – you'll probably have a piece of fiber left over. Then refit the front plate – use a hot glue gun to attach it if you had to cut the canister open. The filters will screen out any particles or droplets that get sucked into the canister, then the charcoal will absorb any toxic gases. The last layer of fiber just stops the charcoal being sucked into the mask.

That's the easy way, but what if you can't get your hands on an industrial mask? Or what if you have one but can't find spare canisters for it? If there's a risk of poison gases being released you're still going to need some sort of protection. Improvised defenses against riot gases like CS – wet bandannas and that sort of thing – won't be much help against industrial chemicals, and they are no use at all against a proper chemical weapon like phosgene or a nerve agent. You absolutely need the protection that activated charcoal, with its ability to absorb and lock up poisons, gives you.

The easiest way to create some protection is with standard disposable dust masks. On their own these will protect you against dust or paint droplets; fit two of them together with a layer of charcoal in between and they'll also filter out poisonous gas. Look for the type with a one-way exhale valve fitted; this will make it much easier to breathe. A box of ten masks can be picked up for less than $10 if you look around.

You won't need the valve on the inner mask, so get a sharp knife and carefully cut around it. The masks will probably have a foam strip to go over your nose; remove that from the outer mask.

Now get about half a cup of powdered activated charcoal and gradually mix in just enough water to form a stiff paste.

Spread the paste all over the inside of the outer mask, keeping the thickness as even as you can.

Be careful not to get any on the valve unit – that can stop the valve working properly, so gas gets in. Now carefully place the inner mask inside the outer, making sure not to disturb the charcoal any more than you have to.

With a hot glue gun, seal the edges of the hole in the inner mask to the rim of the valve on the outer one.

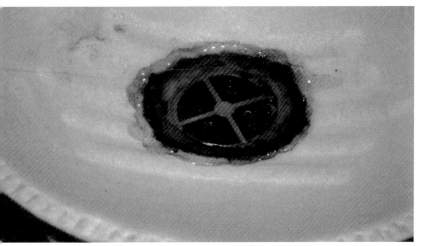

If you don't do this you'll find yourself breathing charcoal dust, which is extremely unpleasant. Now close the gap around the outside of the masks with strips of tape.

Make sure the edges are completely sealed, because if the charcoal gets out you'll lose your protection.

You can use the mask right away if you have to, but it'll be easier to breathe if you can give it a couple of days to dry out.

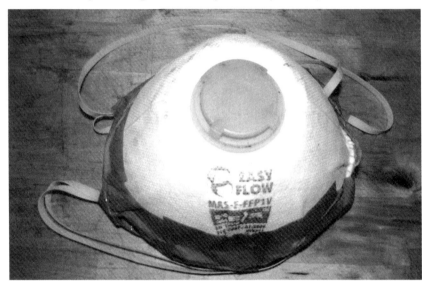

Done? Great. Now make two or three more for each person who needs to be protected.

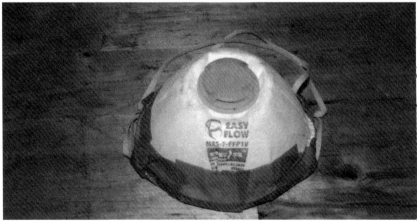

An improvised mask like this won't give as good airflow as a military gas mask, but using a mask with an exhale valve will help a lot.

Wearing one, you should be able to breathe in a gas-contaminated environment for four to six hours, depending on how heavy the contamination is.

A warning though – it depends a lot on what gas we're dealing with. Activated charcoal isn't effective against hydrogen cyanide (HCN), for example; the gas quickly makes the charcoal ineffective. Soviet chemical artillery doctrine called for an attack with HCN to destroy gas mask filters, followed rapidly by nerve agent to do the killing.

You'll know if HCN is getting through your mask; if you feel dizzy, suffer headaches and weakness, start to become confused or find it hard to breathe, you're suffering the early effects.

If this happens close your eyes, hold your breath, and as quickly as you can take off the mask and put on a new one. The good news about HCN is it disperses quickly, so if you can survive for a few minutes you'll be fine – but you will need more than one mask to last that long.

Other chemicals will eventually overload the filter, although it can take hours; if you start to pick up a chemical smell, or feel any symptoms, change your mask.

In any case your first priority should be to get out of the contaminated area as quickly as possible. Soldiers have to hold their position even if it's been soaked in persistent nerve agents; you don't, so you can get away with lighter protective gear.

Remember that many poisonous gases will also affect your eyes, so pair your improvised gas mask with goggles. Safety goggles – not safety glasses – will do, but check for ventilation slots on the surround. If they're ventilated seal the slots with tape or hot glue. It's better to have googles that steam up a bit than goggles that let gas in.

Some chemical weapons – nerve and blister agents, for example – are delivered as liquids. This is spread as droplets, either from an aircraft spray tank or by a bursting charge in a bomb or shell.

The droplets evaporate to give off gas, but they're also harmful if they get on your skin – a single drop of nerve agent on the skin is enough to kill. If you can, stay under cover with your mask on during an attack.

In case you have to go out get some disposable rain capes. These cost a couple of dollars for a pack of five, and they'll keep liquid agents away from your skin long enough for you to get into cover.

For extra protection, use garbage bags held on with tape to cover your feet and legs. After a liquid attack discard anything that might have been contaminated; double-bag and bury it, if you can – *don't* burn it, because you might release toxic vapor.

Poisonous gas – especially a chemical weapon – is nasty stuff and *extremely* dangerous. Even trained soldiers with state of the art protective gear will take casualties. Even a simple mask will give you a much better chance of survival, though. The one shown here is crude, but the British Army – probably the world's leaders at chemical defense – used something similar during the Cold War, so troops could take their standard masks off for a while and still be reasonably well protected.

HOW TO MAKE A WATER FILTER USING ACTIVATED CHARCOAL

- By Claude Davis -

"Preparedness, when properly pursued, is a way of life, not a sudden, spectacular program."

— *By Spencer W. Kimball*

In almost any situation, safe drinking water is the number one priority. Without that, it doesn't matter how much food you have stockpiled and how prepared you are to defend your property. If you don't have water you're going to be dead in a week. The problem is that the infrastructure most of us get our water from is terrifyingly vulnerable to a SHTF scenario.

If your water comes from the municipal supply it comes via a treatment plant, and that plant is going to stop working as soon as its staff quit. If society breaks down the water coming out your faucets might look the same, but the chances are it's going to be untreated. If you have an artesian well you might be lucky, but then you might not. A lot of potential disasters can contaminate the groundwater the well draws from. A nuclear or chemical attack, or a bad industrial accident, will spread contamination; rain will flush

293

that down into the aquifers. In an SHTF situation you can't rely on any water that hasn't been filtered.

In fact it's worse than that. A lot of chemical contaminants will dissolve in water, so a sand or textile filter won't get them out. What's needed is a filter that doesn't just trap particles, but captures molecules of dangerous substances. The solution is activated charcoal.

Activated charcoal can absorb hundreds of times its own weight of contamination, and the finer it's ground the more it can absorb. If you can filter your water through activated charcoal almost all chemicals will be removed from it – even the radioactive particles in fallout.

Your active charcoal filter should be one of the final stages in a multi-layer filtration process. You can just run water straight from source into a charcoal filter if you like, and it'll produce safe water, but you'll go through charcoal a lot faster than you have to. The filter will quickly get choked up with sediment and debris. It's much better to use gravel and sand to do the basic filtration, clearing out debris and large particles, then run the semi-treated water through the charcoal filter to remove toxic chemicals. Finally, because some bacteria and viruses can make it through, use UV sterilization to kill them. This is simple – just put the filtered water in clear plastic containers and leave it in the sun for a day.

You can buy activated carbon filters, and it's always a good idea to keep a stock of them, but what if the crisis goes on long enough that you run out? Or what if there's very heavy contamination and you need to change them a lot more often? That's when you need to be able to make your own.

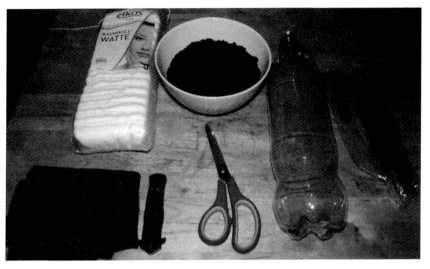

The first thing you need is a container that will hold the filter. This needs to be food grade (so it won't add any more contamination to the water) and large enough that the water's own weight will force it through the filter. The obvious, and cheap, solution is a plastic drink bottle. Water bottles are fine; soda bottles are better because they tend to be stiffer and more robust - they're built to take pressure.

What you're aiming to do is create a deep enough layer of charcoal for the water to pass through. The quantity of charcoal is important – if there isn't enough its ability to soak up contamination will quickly be used up – but the depth matters too. A ton of activated charcoal in a thin layer will be less effective than a pound of it in a deep column. Activated charcoal filters don't just trap pieces of contamination the way a cloth or sand filter does; they actually use chemical reactions to remove toxic substances at a molecular level. That means it's important to keep the water in contact with the charcoal long enough for the reactions to take place, and the easiest way to do that is by creating a deep layer.

If you're using something like a Coke bottle for your filter, there's a simple way to create a deeper layer – just turn the bottle upside down. The narrow neck will give more depth for the same amount of charcoal. At the other end you can either cut away the whole base to make it easy to pour water in, or modify it to suit your water storage system. If you run water through a sand filter then into a barrel with a tap, you can make a filter that fits onto the tap. If water goes from your sand filter into a pipe you can put the charcoal filter on the end of the pipe.

Once you have a suitable bottle you need to add the actual filter. The key here is to make sure the charcoal is properly contained. If it isn't, particles of it will be washed out of the filter and into your clean water. This won't do you any harm, but the filter will slowly lose effectiveness - plus anything you cook with the water will be

kind of gritty. Because you'll be using the smallest particles of charcoal you can, whatever you use to contain it with will need to be a filter itself.

There are two ways to do this.

The First Method

Make a bag from tightly knit fabric and loosely fill it with charcoal.

Then securely close it, either by stitching the top closed or with a tightly knotted cord. Then just put the bag into the bottle through the hole you cut in the base and ram it down tightly into the neck end.

This is quick and easy, but it's not a perfect solution. It should filter the water pretty well, but there's a good chance some of it will be wicked down through the fabric without ever coming in contact with the charcoal. That means it's possible some contamination could make it through, which obviously isn't good news.

Ideally you want the charcoal to be in contact with the walls of the bottle all the way round. That way there's no way any water can get past it — every drop will have to filter its way through.

The Second Method

The first stage is to plug the neck of the bottle so water can get through, but charcoal can't. This is simple — just stuff a cotton ball into the neck, then secure it.

A small piece of cloth held over the mouth of the bottle with a zip tie will do nicely.

Now you have to add the activated charcoal.

Just pour it in the base of the bottle until there's at least three inches of it on top of the cotton, then tap the neck of the bottle on a hard surface to settle it down.

The final stage is to secure the top of the charcoal.

Otherwise, when water is poured into the filter the charcoal will be stirred up and mixed with it; the water won't be properly filtered, because it doesn't have to slowly trickle down through the full depth of charcoal.

Again, use a piece of cloth for this.

Cut out a circle about an inch wider than the bottle and lay it on top of the charcoal.

Now get a half-inch-wide strip of springy plastic – you can cut this from another bottle – and curl it into a circle.

Place that on top of the cloth and let it uncurl, so it traps the cloth between itself and the sides of the bottle.

Before loading the charcoal into your filter, weigh it. This will give you a good idea how long the filter will last. An ounce of charcoal should be good for about 100 gallons of water that's already been through a sand filter – so if you used half a pound of charcoal, the filter will purify 800 gallons before it needs to be rebuilt or replaced. It's worth making at least two filters, and rebuilding used ones as soon as you swap them out, so you'll always have a fresh one ready to do.

It's even better to make more than that and have a couple of spares handy. Of course, you can make as many as you want. You know how to make and activate your own charcoal, so the key ingredient is easily available and cheap. There's no reason for you ever to run out of safe water!

HOW TO MAKE ACTIVATED CHARCOAL PILLS FOR INTOXICATIONS AND STOMACH ACHES

- By Claude Davis -

"Better to have, and not need, than to need, and not have."

— By Franz Kafka

Activated charcoal has many uses in a SHTF situation, but even when life is going on at a normal pace it's useful stuff to have around. You might not need to build a filter to obtain safe drinking water but there are always risks in the world that activated charcoal can help protect you from – anything from insect bites to food poisoning. If you have a supply about the house you can react to these situations quickly and effectively.

Most often, activated charcoal is swallowed to deal with wind or some kind of poisoning. You could keep a jar of it handy and dig in with a spoon when you need some charcoal, but that's messy and unpleasant. It's much better to store it like other medicines – in a handy pill form.

Tablets Or Capsules?

There are two ways you can make activated charcoal pills at home. One is to form it into tablets, but this is quite complicated. Firstly, you need a binder material. This can be bought from a lot of health food suppliers, and it's pretty popular in the illegal drug trade too. Pill binder is a powder that, if it's compressed, binds to itself; mix it with your active ingredient (charcoal in this case), put it in a pill die and apply strong pressure. What comes out is a tablet.

The biggest problem is that you need to use quite a lot of binder – usually at least twice as much as the actual ingredient of the tablet. If you used this method to make charcoal pills you'd have to make 300mg tablets to get 100mg of activated charcoal in each one.

Cost is another problem. The binder itself isn't cheap – expect to pay at least $30 for a one pound bag – and then you'll need a pill die. Simple hand-held ones start at around $80 but these are very slow and fiddly. For each pill you need to measure out the right amount of powder, pour it into the die, knock the top punch down with a hammer and extract the tablet. Then you start all over again.

Making a small bottle of tablets will take you a couple of hours, easily. You can get automatic pill makers that will turn out a few dozen every minute, but they usually cost a couple of thousand dollars – and ordering one might put you on a DEA watch list.

A much easier solution is to make capsules. This doesn't need any specialist equipment or materials (apart from the capsules themselves), it's simple and relatively quick.

All you have to do is get your hands on a bag of empty gelatin capsules and you're good to go. These come in different sizes, but

Size 0 is good for activated charcoal; it's big enough to hold a decent dose, without being too large to swallow easily. You can find them on eBay for less than $10 per thousand.

Capsules have other advantages too. If someone is bitten or stung by an insect you can break the capsule open and use its contents externally to draw out the venom and ease the pain. This isn't possible if you've made tablets.

Preparing Your Charcoal

For medicinal use your best option is to buy food grade charcoal powder. Of course, that's fine as long as society – and the internet – is up and running. If the S has HTF, on the other hand, you're going to have to make your own.

Never make activated charcoal from BBQ charcoal – either lump wood or briquettes. "Charcoal" briquettes usually contain little or no charcoal; they're mostly made of coal dust held together with a clay binder, and impregnated with petrochemicals to help them light more easily. Lump wood charcoal actually is charcoal, but it's also usually treated with chemicals and it certainly isn't food grade.

Don't include any treated timber when you're making your charcoal – no painted siding or old creosoted fence posts. Natural toxins like those found in walnut will be cooked out as the wood chars, but some man-made chemicals can leave nasty residues.

When you activate the charcoal it's important to use clean utensils and wash the final product thoroughly before drying it, to flush out any traces of calcium chloride. The chemical isn't toxic but it is extremely salty, and if you're trying to treat a stomach upset it won't help.

It's also important to grind the charcoal as fine as possible.

The smaller the particles the more effective it will be – and the less you'll have to swallow. A mortar and pestle is the best way to get it really fine; work with small batches and grind it until it's reduced to dust.

Once the charcoal is ready, all you have to do is fill the capsules.

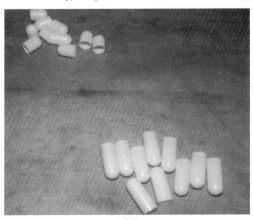

Just use a folded piece of paper to scoop up some of the powder, pour it into the body of the capsule until it's full, then fit the cap and press it down until it clicks.

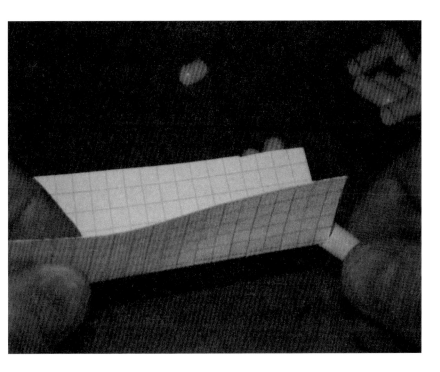

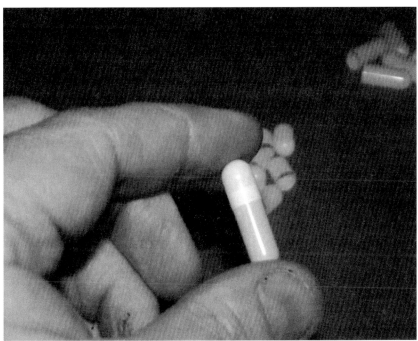

Store the finished capsules in a medicine bottle to protect them from moisture.

When To Use Them

Some people recommend taking activated charcoal regularly as a "detox". This is not a good idea. If you take it regularly it will absorb a lot of the nutrients from your food, leaving you with the fat and calories. Regular use can also cause constipation, which you probably want to avoid (but if you have diarrhea, activated charcoal can help with that).

A good time to break out the charcoal capsules is when you're suffering from wind. This is an irritating condition, but one or two charcoal capsules will absorb the stomach chemicals that generate gas. Don't forget to take the capsules with plenty of water; that will help avoid constipation.

Where your capsules will really earn their keep is when you or someone else has swallowed something poisonous – whether it's a chemical or tainted food. Activated charcoal is so absorbent that it will soak up any poisons that are still in the stomach. It won't be able to affect any that's already got into the rest of the body, but by collecting the rest it reduces the total dose. That can make all the difference between mild symptoms and a serious emergency. Obviously the sooner the charcoal is swallowed the more poison it can safely capture, so it should be taken as possible after you suspect poisoning.

In fact the best way to take activated charcoal is as a series of smaller doses. If you've used Size 0 capsules each of them will contain about half a gram of charcoal. If the victim is an adult they should take four right away, then another four every ten minutes until either the symptoms start to fade or they get to medical help.

Remember that charcoal won't do anything about any poison that's already made it into the body; it can only absorb what's still in the stomach and digestive tract. If possible you should get medical attention if you think someone's been poisoned.

As long as you keep your activated charcoal capsules dry and in a sealed container they should last just about forever. The gelatin capsules will keep the charcoal away from any contamination in the air, and your home-made medicine will always be ready when you need it.

HOW NORTHERN CALIFORNIA NATIVE AMERICANS BUILD THEIR SEMI-SUBTERRANEAN ROUNDHOUSE

- By Erik Bainbridge -

"It wasn't raining when Noah built the Ark."

— Howard Ruff

When most people think of Native American life as it was in the old days, they commonly think of a nomadic tribe living in tipis and having a warrior tradition. However, this is a stereotype that wasn't always true. There was a wide variety of Native American cultures and languages in North America, with some very different ways of life.

Native Americans living in coastal California just north of today's San Francisco couldn't have been more different than that stereotype. Living in stable villages in homes made of materials such as tule reeds or redwood bark, each village lived within its own territory. There was no warrior tradition or warrior class. They had no need to be migratory. Food was generally abundant except during drought years. Salmon spawned in coastal waterways, deer and other game were plentiful, and year-round streams provided water. Before Europeans arrived in the late 18th century, life had been stable there for millennia.

If you could travel back in time to before Europeans first colonized California and visited a typical village in this area, you'd likely notice two or more hills in the village. The hills would usually be perfectly round in shape, although they could be oval in some villages. You might see smoke coming out of the hills. If you walked closer, you'd see the smoke was coming from a hole on the hill and that each hill had at least one entrance.

The hills were man made. The smaller hill(s) would be one or more sweathouses, and the large hill would be the village roundhouse. All were semi-subterranean and made by digging a hole in the ground, building a roof over it, and covering the roof with earth. The roundhouse served as a communal hall, a dance house, and a ceremonial house. The exact usages could vary regionally.

In the 19th and early 20th centuries, construction changed. In some cases, the earthen roof was replaced with shakes. In most cases, roundhouse construction evolved to be entirely above ground, which is how most roundhouses are built today. There aren't many accounts of the exact architecture of the old semi-subterranean roundhouses; one of the most useful is *Miwok Material Culture: Indian Life of the Yosemite Region* by S. A. Barrett and E. W. Gifford. This chapter is based on information in this book and on my own experience in rebuilding and maintaining a modern-day semi-subterranean roundhouse that was built in the traditional way.

Another excellent source of information is *Ethnographic Notes on California Indian Tribes* by C. Hart Merriam. Most of the roundhouses Merriam describes are aboveground styles that emerged beginning in the late 19th century after California became a state and people began using the modern building materials and tools of the Americans now swarming into the new state.

None of the original semi-subterranean roundhouses have survived. Wood decays quickly underground, so a roundhouse lasts at most a few decades.

Perhaps for this reason, some villages had a tradition of burning the roundhouse after the headman died and building a new one to replace it. However, there are contemporary recreations.

One is at the Chaw'se Indian Grinding Rock State Historic Park near Jackson, California, another is in the Indian village of the Ahwahnee in Yosemite National Park, and a third is in the replica Coast Miwok village Kule Loklo ("Bear Valley") in California's Point Reyes National Seashore. All three are in state or federal parks but are used in traditional ways by California native people.

Kule Loklo[22] was created in the 1970s when a group of educators and archeologists in Marin County formed the Miwok Archeological Preserve of Marin (MAPOM) and partnered with the National Park Service to build a replica Coast Miwok Indian village.

The original 1970s roundhouse no longer stands, but you can visit the replacement that was constructed in 1992.

---

[22] *Kule Loklo roundhouse entrance - photo by Erik Gordon Bainbridge*

The roundhouse is customarily kept locked, but you may be able to see the interior during Kule Loklo's annual Big Time, usually held the third Saturday in July, when you can also watch traditional Pomo Indian dancing in the dance circle under a towering bay laurel tree outside.

The Park also provides guided tours of Kule Loklo for adults and education programs for school children.

Photographs are not allowed inside the completed roundhouse.

The following is a photograph of the interior[23] of the sweathouse at Kule Loklo, which is much smaller than the roundhouse but has a similar construction.

---

[23] *Kule Loklo Sweathouse interior - photo by Erik Gordon Bainbridge*

Building the Semi-Subterranean Roundhouse

The first step in building a roundhouse is to dig out the pit that will become its floor.

It's a labor-intensive task that's hard work even today, but it was even more difficult in the days when there were no shovels or metal tools and all digging had to be done using fire-hardened digging sticks and abalone shells.

The original roundhouse at Kule Loklo was constructed this way by dedicated volunteers in the 1970s, but most work on the current roundhouse has been done using modern tools.

When the pit is dug, the sides are tapered so that the floor is smaller than at ground level.

Traditional roundhouses ranged from about 30 feet to about 60 feet in diameter. Barrett states that in the Yosemite region, the diameter of the pit to be dug for the roundhouse was measured by four men lying on the ground head to foot, which he estimates to be about 44 feet.

At Kule Loklo, the roundhouse has a 40-foot floor diameter. The walls of the roundhouse are below ground and taper inward and have rocks laid into them.

The roundhouse's floor is earthen. Merriam reports that traditionally some villages mixed acorn flour—and later sometimes wheat flour—into the wet earth to form a hard surface when it dried. This reduced the dust kicked up into the air when people were dancing.

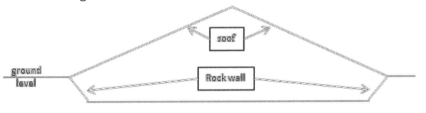

roundhouse cross section (not to scale)

Supporting Poles

Selecting the poles that support the roundhouse is the most challenging task. They need to be sturdy, of course, and ideally a wye (naturally forked). If not a wye, then the top end will have be notched to support the cross beams. They will support the roundhouse for decades. It's crucial to find the right ones, but finding them can be daunting, and in the old days, carrying them back to the village was not a task for the weak.

Barrett reports that there were two sets of poles supporting the roof: an inner set of four thick poles and an outer set of eight thinner poles. At Kule Loklo, there are twelve outer poles.

Barrett describes the four inner poles as being oak, a foot in diameter, separated by the length of a man's reach, and sunk in a hole two feet in depth. This is similar to Kule Loklo except that the inner four poles are 9.5 feet apart. Barrett doesn't give the distance between the outer poles; at Kule Loklo, they are about seven feet apart.

In the roundhouse that Barrett describes, the two rear center poles were special. They were treated with traditional medicine, and only the dancers were allowed to come near them. There is no center pole in this roundhouse.

The Kule Loklo roundhouse is different. It has a large center pole, but contrary to what most visitors think, its function is not to support the roof. Its role is ceremonial, similar to the rear poles that Barrett describes.

Roof Construction

With the posts erected, the next step is to put the horizontal poles in place. These form the ceiling of the roundhouse and extend from ground level to the center. Barrett reports that they were three to five inches in diameter and were made of buckeye or willow.

At Kule Loklo, they are Douglas fir. A large crew of volunteers[24] spent nearly a year stripping bark from them using draw knives.

After the poles are in place, protective material needs to be added before covering it with earth to block rain from seeping through. In the old days, brush was used for this layer. Barrett describes a roundhouse in which four layers of brush were used for this.

The lower two layers were willow branches at 90 degree angles to each other. The third layer was of closely packed twigs, and finally, a layer of either digger or western pine needles were added (Barrett specifies that sugar pine needles were never avoided).

---

[24] *Federated Indians of Graton Rancheria and Park volunteers stripping bark from Douglas fir poles for Kule Loklo roundhouse roof – photo by Erik Gordon Bainbridge*

The top layer was earth and was four to five inches in depth. The total roof thickness after all layers were added was one and a half to two feet.

At Kule Loklo, several layers of tarp to block water and a layer of wire mesh to block rodents from digging through replaced the brush and pine needles. The earth on the roof is about three to five inches thick. It hasn't been entirely successful however.

The roundhouse was originally built in 1992, and the roof was completely rebuilt in 2005, both times using several layers of tarps to protect the Douglas fir roof poles. Despite this, some of tarps had to be replaced in the late 1990s, and the roundhouse still leaks in heavy rains despite the tarps.

It's important for the posts and all roof poles to be debarked before installing them; leaving the bark on invites insects and dramatically shortens its useful life.

Roundhouse Entrance

There are different styles for the roundhouse entrance. I've been told that in the very old days, many roundhouses didn't even have doors or entrances as we think of them today. Entrance and exit was through the smoke hole. After the fire started, no one left until the fire died down. I haven't seen any written descriptions of these however.

All the roundhouses that I've read formal accounts about had at least one entrance other than the smoke hole. In some cases, the entrance was simply an opening in the roundhouse roof and an excavation or depression in the surrounding ground. In many cases, such as at Kule Loklo, there is an entrance vestibule. Kule Loklo's is about 24 feet long and about eight feet wide. The sides are redwood bark. The roof is earth-covered.

Fire Pit

The ideal location for the fire pit is in the center of the roundhouse. This allows the smoke hole to be at the high point of the roof, which reduces how much smoke builds up inside the roundhouse. Most traditional roundhouses I've read about have had a center fire pit.

However, some roundhouses, such as the one at Kule Loklo, have a center pole, which necessitates placing the fire pit elsewhere. In the Kule Loklo roundhouse, the fire pit is between the center pole and the entrance.

The smoke hole needs to be directly over the fire pit for fire safety reasons; however, the absence of a central smoke hole allows smoke to build up at the roof's peak and causes the roundhouse to fill with smoke quickly if the fire turns smoky. One solution to this might be to enlarge and lengthen the smoke hole toward the center.

The Kule Loklo roundhouse was built with just one entrance, facing east, but several years after its construction, a 28" x 56"opening was added on the west side to aid with airflow and to reduce smoke. Smoke reduction is a problem with any indoor fire, especially in a structure without a chimney, like the roundhouse. There are several steps you can take to minimize smoke.

The most fundamental is to use only high-quality wood. Oak and madrone are best for this, but make sure it's dry and seasoned. Wet or green wood will smoke more. If it's properly seasoned, you should see small cracks forming in the firewood cross section. One risk in using low-quality wood is getting a pitch log. This is usually pine log with a large amount of resin in it.

It's heavier than a regular pine long, can burn like a torch, and emits black smoke. If you accidentally put one on the fire in the roundhouse, the only thing to do is to remove it immediately with a shovel and extinguish it. Otherwise, the roundhouse will quickly fill with smoke. Burning a very hot fire in the roundhouse for several hours before an event will also help reduce smoke. You need a large pile of hot coals in the fire. After the event starts, you can reduce the size of the fire. Cleaning out the fire pit before each event is also essential. If you have ash and cinders left over from previous fires, you will probably have a smoky fire.

Summary

Building a roundhouse like the ones traditionally used by Northern California's Miwok and Pomo people before the twentieth century, as a semi-subterranean structure with an earthen roof, is a huge amount of work. This is why most roundhouses today are constructed on a smaller scale, for a family or two maybe.

Here's a quick illustration of a DIY semi-subterranean house:

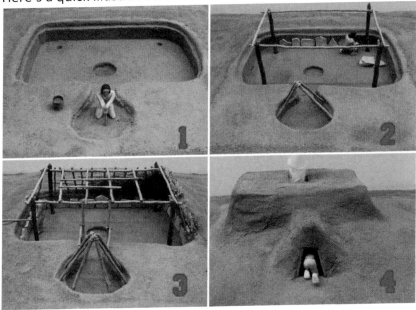

The temperature is always moderate inside—mild on cold winter days and cool on hot summer days—and the earthen walls and roof isolate the interior from the noises outside.

Anyone attempting to build one needs to pay particular attention to debarking the poles, to waterproofing the roof, and to reducing smoke.

HOW THE SHERIFFS FROM THE FRONTIERS DEFENDED THEIR VILLAGES AND TOWNS

- By Ruff Simons -

"If we desire to avoid insult, we must be able to repel it; if we desire to secure peace, one of the most powerful instruments of our rising prosperity, it must be known that we are at all times ready for War."

— *George Washington*

Westerns give us a vivid picture of law enforcement in the Old West. When a gang of outlaws starts to terrorize a town, the frightened inhabitants beg their sheriff to do something—but usually he's either corrupt, a coward, or just not up to the job.

Everything seems lost until an enigmatic stranger appears, confronts the troublemakers, and saves the day. It's a striking image—but it's wrong in almost every detail.

The people who settled the West were not shrinking violets. The fact that they were out there in the first place should tell us that. These were people who'd left their homes and traveled—

322

sometimes from the cities of the East Coast and often all the way from Europe—to make a new life in uncharted wilderness.

They were pioneers and adventurers—bold, determined people. They may have lived in towns, but in most cases, they had built those towns themselves—few western settlements at the time had seen two generations raised there, and many were only a few years old. Even recent arrivals had struck out on a long, tough, and often dangerous journey to reach their new home, and not many of them were easily scared.

Then there were the lawmen. Movies and novels often mix up the roles of marshal and sheriff, but they were very different. The history of the Old West mostly played out in territories that hadn't yet achieved statehood.

That meant there were no state governments to take care of law enforcement.

The federal government's response was to send U.S. marshals into the new territories. The United States Marshals Service is the country's oldest law  enforcement agency and was set up in 1789 as the enforcement arm of the federal courts. Marshals were ideal for the job because they had extensive powers; they could hire local deputies or recruit a posse. Virgil Earp was a U.S. Marshal, and he hired Wyatt Earp (picture) and Doc Holliday as assistants.

But while marshals had a lot of power, there weren't many of them—certainly not enough to cover the huge and growing expanses of the West.

As towns became established, they started to take responsibility for their own law enforcement in the shape of local sheriffs. The office of sheriff is an ancient one dating back to Saxon England, but in the West, it took on a distinctive form. Instead of an official appointed by the king, these new sheriffs were elected by the townspeople and given responsibility for law and order. Because they were elected, sheriffs tended to be trusted. There were exceptions however—elections could be rigged, or enough voters could be bribed to elect an unpopular candidate—but in general, the job was given to someone the people thought could do it.

The position came with a lot of power and even more responsibility. The sheriff could appoint deputies to help him with his duties, which were many. Sheriffs also often acted as tax collectors and resolved disputes over grazing rights or access to water. They're most famous as lawmen though.

In the early days, before the western territories achieved statehood, sheriffs literally had the power of life and death. A sheriff could arrest wrongdoers, hold a trial, and carry out the sentence. Sometimes that meant locking a drunk up in the town jail for a few days; sometimes it meant a hanging.

Crime in the West

What kinds of crimes did those sheriffs have to deal with though? Another stereotype we get from movies is that the Old West was a lawless, violent place. The truth is, in general, it wasn't.

In fact, a typical Western town in the 1860s had a lot less crime and disorder than it does today. That's mostly down to the people who lived there and the lives they led. The new lands of the West attracted a wide range of personalities, from visionaries that dreamed of building a paradise to misfits on the run from the law to families, but the untamed land was a ruthless judge.

To survive more than a few weeks out there, never mind to successfully establish a farm or business, you had to learn to work together. Neighbors helped each other by trading supplies or lending muscle to a building project. Merchants gave credit on an honor system, and those who abused that trust soon found themselves unwelcome in town.

After the Civil War, the ranks of the pioneers swelled with veterans, who brought their own camaraderie with them.

All this meant a level of trust soon developed in a Western town. People knew their neighbors; they worked beside them and socialized with them. They knew they could rely on each other for help. In this atmosphere, petty crime was frowned on, and violence was surprisingly rare.

When violence threatened, it usually came from outside. There were gangs of outlaws that were often made up of men who'd failed to fit in with the frontier society and banded together with others like them. As big ranchers moved in and came into conflict with small farmers, they sometimes hired gangs of gunslingers to enforce their will.

Later the early railway barons would resort to the same tactics. When the federal government began its war against the Plains Indians, the previous good relations between settlers and the tribes broke down, and warriors began attacking farms and even small towns.

In fact, the threats that faced those old-time lawmen were a lot like the ones you're likely to be dealing with in a SHTF scenario, but they're probably going to fall on you a lot quicker.

After all, in the West, society was still being built, home by home and farm by farm. The majority of the people were part of that effort. They were used to taking care of themselves, growing their own food, digging wells for water, and resolving disputes like adults.

Now imagine what it will be like when a developed society like ours, full of people that think meat grows in shrink-wrapped packages, collapses. Suddenly all those people have to fend for themselves—and unlike the old pioneers, they don't have any idea how to do it. It won't be long before marauding gangs, desperate for basic necessities like food and water, are trying to take them from anyone who looks like they're managing to cope with the situation.

Existing law enforcement probably won't be able to help you much. either. What elements of it haven't collapsed will be completely overwhelmed because chaos will spread far and fast. If you want to protect yourself, your family, and your property in this scenario, you're going to have to do it yourself.

Many people in the USA now realize this and aim to be prepared, but a lot of them are going the wrong way about it. This is where the lessons of those old sheriffs come in.   To apply the same techniques as sheriffs in the West used, it helps to look at how your own situation resembles theirs—and how it's different.

Equipment

Guns

The USA's high rate of gun ownership is what makes it possible to defend your community if society breaks down—but it also increases the threat. You can bet that any group of marauders will quickly pick up every gun they can get their hands on, while hungry refugees could also be carrying to defend themselves. Having the right guns available is going to make a huge difference to your efforts to preserve a little patch of law.

Colt still calls their Single Action Army revolver—the famous Peacemaker—"The gun that won the West." It wasn't. In fact, the role of handguns in the Old West has been hugely exaggerated, something else we can thank Hollywood for. Yes, many famous figures from that time carried one, but they were nowhere near as common as the movies make out.

Almost every household on the frontier was armed, but guns were expensive—compared to the average income, a lot more expensive than they are now—and few people could afford a collection of them. They tended to buy one gun and would pick one that would be as versatile as possible. Usually, it wasn't a revolver.

For the typical settler in one of the new American territories, a handgun wasn't actually good for much. He needed a gun to put food on the table, maybe to hunt animals for their pelts, and to keep critters away from his crops. Self-defense was just something else it could be used for if necessary, but few people saw that as their gun's main function, and if they did use it for protection, it was more likely to be against an animal than a person.

The popular image of every cowboy and rancher walking around with a six-shooter strapped to his hip simply isn't correct, as period photos show. Some did carry revolvers, but most didn't. Rifles were far more common weapons in the West because they could be used for hunting and had a longer range. After the Civil War, there was no shortage of military-surplus rifle muskets, and many settlers carried those or similar weapons.

If there really is a gun that won the West, though, it has to be the humble 12-gauge shotgun. It's hard to imagine a more versatile workhorse firearm than this. It can be loaded with anything from a single massive projectile—ball then, slug now—to a charge of rock salt, so it's capable of bringing down most game. Anything from small birds to the largest deer can be taken with an appropriately loaded shotgun.

THE LOST WAYS

It's also ideal for self-defense at short and medium range. No pistol cartridge comes close to the power of a 12-gauge, and loaded with buckshot, it also has a much longer effective range. Familiarity plays a part since in an emergency you'll be a lot better off with the gun you carry and use every day, but unless you've done hundreds of hours of specialist police or military handgun training, a shotgun is just an easier weapon to protect yourself with.

The same things that made a shotgun the ideal weapon in the 19th century West still hold true today; in fact, if anything, its advantages have increased. There's a wider choice of ammunition than ever, including rifled slugs that are accurate and hard-hitting out to 100 yards or more. Traditional side-by-sides have been replaced with pump actions, which are extremely reliable but offer higher ammunition capacity.

Shotguns are designed for rapid, instinctive aiming and are useful for hunting and a critical advantage in a self-defense situation. They also have a huge psychological effect. The sound of a pump shotgun chambering a round is instantly recognizable and highly intimidating. Cops will tell you that it often makes intruders turn tail and run without a single shot being fired.

If it's SHTF time, a lot of the intruders you'll be facing are starving refugees from the city. You don't want them stealing your supplies, but you don't want to shoot them either if you can avoid it.

Communications

It's amazing how quickly we've become used to today's hyper-connected world. Most of us are never out of touch, wherever we are, but only 25 years ago cell phones were a rarity and mobile Internet completely unheard of. If you wanted to talk to someone while you were out, you found a pay phone and hoped they were at home.

In the Old West, even that option didn't exist. There were no telephones, and the only quick way of communicating over long distances was the embryonic telegraph system.

The first telegraph line went up in 1844, linking Washington, D.C., with Baltimore. By 1856 there were around 40 U.S. telegraph companies, all based in the eastern states, but one of them, which had recently renamed itself Western Union, had begun buying up many of the others. Western Union opened the first transcontinental line in 1861 between New York and California, and through the rest of the century, the telegraph network slowly spread through the developing West.

Not every town had a telegraph station though, and few had more than one. Sending a message wasn't a fast process. Each one had to be tapped out by hand using Morse code then written down at the receiving end. Then either the person it was addressed to had to pick it up at the telegraph station or a Western Union runner would deliver it.

Even so, it was a huge improvement over what went before: – the Pony Express. Riders on fast horses, changing mounts frequently, could carry a 20-pound sack of mail from St. Joseph, Missouri, to Sacramento, California, in around ten days. The Pony Express became a legend of the West—but it closed two days after the transcontinental telegraph started operating. Still, riders were the quickest way to get a message between most towns out west until well into the 1880s unless you lived beside the railroad.

If society collapses, you'll suddenly find your communication options at least as narrow as those of a 19th century pioneer. Cell phones, landline exchanges, and the Internet will go down quickly. The only modern communications that will work are self-contained radios with their own power sources, and if you don't have them in your SHTF kit, you'll be back to using riders to carry messages outside your local area. If you don't have any horses and have to rely on automobiles or motorbikes, that's going to use valuable fuel reserves you're probably reluctant to waste, but good communication played a big part in keeping the Old West law abiding, and they're just as important for you.

Organization

That brings us on to the next key point: how to organize. That's something a lot of preppers seem to overlook. A big part of being ready for when the SHTF is self-reliance, and that doesn't seem to sit well with committee meetings and organizing communities to work together, but it needs to be talked about.

The people who set out to build the West were also self-reliant; they had to be. But they also knew they could accomplish more by working together than they could as individuals.

One family can secure and defend their own property, but they have no control over the surrounding area, and if a large enough group of marauders attacks them, they're eventually going to be overrun. A loose community of hundreds of well-prepared, self-reliant people could be taken down by a dozen bandits if they only have to deal with them one or two or five at a time. Now imagine the same dozen robbers approaching a typical 19th century town out on the frontier.

The town probably only had a couple of hundred people, and they lacked most of the advantages we have today. They had no radios and no motor vehicles, and the most common firearms were double-barrel shotguns and single-shot rifle muskets. But the robbers had almost no chance, because the townspeople had an informal but effective organization to keep the peace.

The Sheriff

Frontier towns couldn't support a full-time police department; everyone was too busy taming the surrounding land and building the town itself. Even the sheriff often wasn't a full-time law enforcer. Elected from among the people, he probably had a farm or business of his own to run.

There were upsides to this though. Usually there wasn't a divide between law enforcement and civilians as there often is now. The townspeople knew that the sheriff was one of their own. Most of them had voted for him; the ones who hadn't still knew who he was. There was an essential link between sheriff and people; they'd chosen him to protect them from lawbreakers, and that meant he could count on their support when he needed it.

Sheriffs could call for support in many ways, but one of their most valuable assets was simply the community itself. People talked to their neighbors in a web of information sharing that covered the district. If someone had a problem with pilfering around their farm, pretty soon everyone else would know about it and be on the lookout.

Word would soon get to the sheriff, and he'd probably take a look around the area. Any opportunist criminals would quickly see that the community was on the alert, and that had a big deterrent effect.

Deputy Sheriffs

Where deterrence didn't work, the sheriff had the power to deputize people to help him. Larger towns might have full-time deputies that were paid from the sheriff's share of the taxes he collected. In smaller settlements, the sheriff might have a pool of men he knew he could rely on but would only deputize when they were needed.

That's the situation you'll be in if society collapses; it's not likely your local community will be big enough to support full-time deputies.

A deputy sheriff, then and now, is a person appointed by the sheriff to carry out the sheriff's duties. They have all the powers of the sheriff himself, including investigating crimes, making arrests, and detaining suspects and criminals. Traditionally, a deputy is an employee of the sheriff, meaning they're paid by the sheriff and are under their command.

Posses

Because they had to be paid, the number of deputies a sheriff could employ was limited. One option was to hire them only when needed, but sometimes so much manpower was needed that it just wasn't possible to hire that many people.

That's where another of the sheriff's powers came in: the right to raise a posse. This comes from the tradition of Posse Comitatus, or "power of the community," and like the office of sheriff itself, it goes back to English common law.

A sheriff has the power to conscript any able-bodied man into a posse when manpower is needed. Usually that happened when a fugitive had to be captured or a large group of outlaws threatened the peace.

Members of a posse didn't have all the powers of a sheriff or deputy, but they did have whatever powers the sheriff delegated to them. For example, if the posse was called out for a manhunt, its members would be given the power to arrest the fugitive. Other times the right to self-defense would be enough for the task.

Bringing It Up To Date

So law and order in the Old West was mostly handled by sheriffs and the help they could draw on from their communities, either by appointing deputies or raising a posse. The big question is, when our own society collapses, how can you use those methods to keep yourself and the people around you safe? Is it even an appropriate way to do things?

The answer to that question has to be yes. Sheriffs, unlike most modern police forces, belong to the old tradition of policing by consent. If the people didn't like the job their sheriff was doing, when his term was up, they could elect someone else. That was an important check that kept most sheriffs honest.

Now, with the police increasingly politicized and remote from the people, the element of consent is gone. That doesn't matter much to a powerful government that can enforce its will through force, but what about when that government loses control? If you want to preserve safety in the aftermath, the first thing you need to do is get consent because people aren't going to accept any other form of policing.

Getting yourself elected as sheriff probably isn't realistic in an SHTF scenario. People are likely to be too worried and too involved in looking after themselves to feel like organizing a town hall meeting. Security is a priority though, and it's likely to be needed sooner rather than later.

That means someone has to take on the responsibility. If nobody else is doing it, you're going to have to step up, and your first task is going to be building the consent you need. If you just start patrolling the area with a gun, the chances are you'll be looked at with suspicion—but with the right groundwork, you'll get a much better response.

The first thing to do is speak to as many of your neighbors as you can. If you can get them all together at once, great; if not, talk to them individually. Explain that you're worried about lawlessness affecting you and them and that you have some ideas to help prevent any issues. Some will immediately see the advantages. Others might need some convincing.

Focus on these points:

- ❖ Safety in numbers. A group of people working together can achieve a lot more than the same number all doing their own thing—and that applies to security too.
- ❖ Better awareness. Being organized means sharing information, and that means everyone gets advanced warning of any developing problems.
- ❖ Less time-consuming. If every home is 100% responsible for its own security, everyone will spend a lot of time checking for intruders and standing guard. That wastes time people could use producing food and adapting to the crisis.
- ❖ Safety for singles. Families can take turns checking perimeters at night or standing guard when marauders are around. Anyone living alone can't do that. If there are older

people in your area, they're vulnerable too—and local safety is only as strong as the weakest link.

When you show people that you've thought about keeping the area safe from lawbreakers and you have a plan to do it, most of them are going to agree. You're not trying to take over; you just have some positive suggestions to save everyone some time and gain them some security. What you'll probably find is that your friends and neighbors have been worrying about exactly those issues.

Most of us think we can protect our homes by ourselves—and most of the time we can—but when a dozen armed and desperate people could raid our food supplies at any time, we start to realize that we need to sleep sometime, and that leaves a lot of hours when we're not ready to respond. Ask anyone who's done time in the military how exhausting sentry duty gets.

Once the majority of your neighbors have accepted your plan, you're ready to get started. Without announcing it, you've basically got yourself elected as sheriff. Don't get carried away, but now you need to start putting the plan into effect—and that means you're going to need deputies.

This looks like the tricky bit; you have to persuade people to give up some of their time to help you out. Actually, it's not that hard, though, because they'll see the benefits pretty quickly. In exchange for taking turns at patrolling the area, they'll be able to sleep soundly every other night, knowing that someone's out there keeping an eye on things and ready to raise the alarm if necessary.

Showing the Flag

One of the most important things you can do is have a visible presence around the clock. That's one of the main reasons an old-time sheriff would take on deputies. Many crimes are a lot easier to commit at night, but if the area's being patrolled, that's a big deterrent. Obviously, you can't do it all yourself; you need to sleep too, and you have other things to attend to. So find a few volunteers who can see the benefits, and organize a shift system. These people will do the job of your deputies.

How you patrol will depend a lot on the area. If it's suburban or even urban, you might need to control access. A small neighborhood can be held together even in a major collapse but not if refugees and raiders have easy access.

Then again, you can't mobilize enough manpower to cover every road. Consider barricading most of them, at least well enough to keep vehicles out, and having checkpoints to control the one or two you leave open. A roving deputy can check the others on his rounds to make sure nobody's trying to reopen them.

In a rural community, homes are likely to be a lot more scattered, and distances will be longer. Vehicle patrols are an option here as long as fuel lasts, but outside of town, you're more likely to have access to horses and people that can ride. They're a natural choice for the job.

Anyone that's patrolling should be armed with at least a handgun and ideally a shotgun or rifle, and at night they'll need a flashlight.

If you have radios, they should take one of those too. What you don't want is to have them fully kitted out with military-style tactical gear. They're just guys out looking after their area and their neighbors after all. They just have to be visible enough to be noticed.

Especially during the day, your deputies should be well-known and approachable people. One of the most important things they can do, apart from just being seen, is to talk to everyone they meet. That makes people feel involved in protecting themselves, which means they'll be more supportive of what you're doing. It also helps information flow around, and that's vital. Remember, most of the modern ways of passing on information will be gone, and just like in the Old West, it's all going to be done by face-to-face conversations.

That's another reason for avoiding the military look. It's just psychologically harder to talk to someone that looks ready to fight a war, even if you know them. In the actual military, a lot of soldiers whose job it is to talk to the locals will walk around with no helmet or armor and just a sidearm, even in a high-threat environment. They take a risk—and break the rules—because people are more likely to tell them stuff.

So your deputies need to talk to people, help them out where they can, and do everything in their power to build an atmosphere where people talk about any worries they have, anything they've seen, and anything else that can help preserve law and order.

Don't just look outward either. If someone's suffering from stress—
and people will be in an extreme SHTF scenario—you can pick up
advance warning of any issues that are developing. If someone's
started drinking heavily, getting aggressive with family or
neighbors, or possibly even thinking of suicide, you'll get to hear
about it, and you can keep an eye on the situation before it gets
out of control.

You and your deputies have other things to do too. You'll know the
places in the area where bandits or refugees might hide out. Check
them regularly for signs that anyone's been using them. Also take
a look at anything that could endanger the community. If there's a
levee nearby, make sure it's visited daily—more often in heavy rain.
Make sure nobody's playing around with local industries that use
hazardous chemicals, and check for evidence of tampering with the
water supply.

One of the likeliest challenges you'll face is groups of refugees
looking for food, shelter, and security. You can't take them in; your
own resources, no matter how well prepared you are, will be
stretched enough as the crisis goes on.

Be firm but compassionate. You need to turn them away, but don't
use force unless they do it first. They're Americans, after all, and
they're not to blame for what's happened.

Some of them might even have been prepared for a social
breakdown but had to move out because their home was
threatened or destroyed. Give them what help you can without
eating into your own reserves: directions to safe areas or even
some medical supplies for anyone who's really sick or injured.

Eventually news is going to spread that your community has managed to hold itself together, and no matter how small it is— even if it's just you and one or two neighbors—someone's going to think of trying to take your resources away from you. There's a good chance that when they see you're prepared and vigilant, they'll back off and look for an easier target—but they might not. That's the worst-case scenario, and you need to be prepared for it.

Raising a Posse

When you see a posse in the movies, it's usually been raised to pursue a fugitive. That was certainly one of their functions, but it's not one you're likely to be calling on. Your priority is to keep wrongdoers out of your community. If they run, it's usually best to just let them get away; chasing them uses manpower and resources you can't afford.

But posses had another use, and that was for self-defense against a large group of attackers. That's something you're almost certainly going to need.

Sheriffs in the Old West had a legal right to draft manpower and were backed up by the threat of penalties under Posse comitatus. That's an advantage you won't have. Law will have broken down; you're trying to hold a little piece of it together, but you can't do it by imposing fines on people who won't join your posse. Ten to one they aren't going to pay the fines either. You'll have to use persuasion, and again, most people will see the sense behind it. Those who don't will probably change their minds the first time your posse proves its worth.

Raising a posse isn't something you can leave until the barbarians are at the gates. You have to know who you can call on that will be willing to help. Traditionally, that was all able-bodied men; now it's any able-bodied adult. You have to make sure they all have access to a gun, ideally a long gun. If any don't, see if you can get those with multiple guns to loan one—and make sure the borrower knows how to use it.

Arrange a place for the posse to assemble if gunfire breaks out: somewhere central and easily reached but not in the line of fire from the ways into your neighborhood. If you can and if you have enough people, organize them into teams, and try to spread any veterans among those teams to reinforce them.

When the community comes under attack, the last thing you want is for everyone to rush toward the sound of the guns. What if the raiders have split into two groups? Keep a reserve to deal with anything unexpected. An old sheriff wouldn't take everyone with him; he'd leave at least one trusted deputy and enough men to protect the town while he was gone.

Sheriffs in the Old West had some other powers that you don't. They could convict and imprison or hang lawbreakers. Don't even go there unless it's clear the disaster is permanent. Yes, you could lock someone up in your garage and call it the town jail, but you'd just have to feed them. As for executions, that's very dangerous territory. Even in the worst-case scenario, like a major EMP attack, there's a good chance the government will regain control eventually. If that happens, you don't need questions being asked about what happened during the crisis.

The same goes for lynchings. If you're the one who maintained the law—even unofficially—and a criminal was lynched, you're going to be held responsible for it. When raiders arrive, aim to drive them off. If any get shot in the process, that's legitimate self-defense, but frontier justice is a different story.

Law enforcement in the Old West was all about the community looking after itself. It was based on consent and on power exercised by a sheriff chosen from among the people. That's the way the law should be maintained, and many of today's social problems trace back to the fact that it isn't done that way anymore. After the SHTF, it's going to be different. Surviving communities will have to return to the ways of the Western pioneers because there will be no other way to maintain law and order.

If those communities don't adopt the Western way of keeping the peace, then they won't last. However strong and self-reliant they are, they'll inevitably be overwhelmed, one house at a time, by those who emerge from the wreckage all around them.

The traditions of the sheriff, America's iconic lawman, were essential to building this country. They'll be just as essential to rebuilding it after a collapse.

WILD WEST GUNS FOR SHTF AND A GUIDE TO ROLLING YOUR OWN AMMO

- By Mike Searson -

"The rifle itself has no moral stature, since it has no will of its own. Naturally, it may be used by evil men for evil purposes, but there are more good men than evil, and while the latter cannot be persuaded to the path of righteousness by propaganda, they can certainly be corrected by good men with rifles."

– Jeff Cooper

A true end-of-the-world scenario, with no electricity, power, or other conveniences, could very well transform us into users of 19th century technology.

How likely this scenario could be is a matter of opinion, but it is something that should give us a reason to prepare.

Modern Firearms

Most preppers and survivalists are familiar with the modern standby firearms: Glock, SIG, AR, AK, shotgun, etc. We love them too and always have a few of each on hand, but an unimaginable disaster could render them obsolete rather quickly. A high-end semiauto is a thing of beauty with a stockpile of ammo and the skill in knowing how to use it, but what happens when a part breaks and the factory and all its suppliers are gone?

An amateur gunsmith can make almost any part within reason, but we like to keep a few of the older and more reliable guns that use fewer moving parts and can be repaired at a pre-Industrial Revolution level of technology and tools.

Handguns

One of our favorites in this category is the Ruger Blackhawk line of revolvers.

The Blackhawk was the first major successful clone of Colt's legendary 1873 Single Action Army revolver, aka the "Peacemaker." The revolver in the picture was issued to the U.S. Cavalry early in 1874. Ruger went with a single-piece frame and used modern steel and aluminum in the

(Photo credits: Hmaag).

manufacturing process to build a much stronger revolver than anything Colt ever turned out. In 1977 they introduced the transfer bar in order to make it safe to carry six rounds as opposed to five in the cylinder.

Other improvements included usable adjustable sights and the ability to mount a scope or electronic sight on the revolver. Admittedly, they do not have the graceful, flowing lines of the classic SAA. If you think you need that "look," there is a line called the Vaquero that uses fixed sights but is otherwise the same handgun, although this should not be confused with the "New Vaquero," which is built on a slightly smaller frame.

A Blackhawk, Super Blackhawk, or Vaquero (original or "Old Model," not the "New Vaquero") in 45 Colt can be loaded to pressures exceeding the modern 44 Magnum. Thus, it is capable of taking any game in North America and is effective against two-legged predators as well. These single-action revolvers epitomize strength and will outlive generations of shooters.

Their simple design means they will outperform modern double-action revolvers in the maintenance department, whose lock work is more suited to a watchmaker than an amateur gunsmith too.

They may not have the capacity or ability to reload quickly, but this can be remedied by carrying a pair of them and remembering the "Gunfighter's Motto" of the fastest reload being a second gun.

Rifles

When it comes to a rifle that you want to be able to rely on, you may want to consider a quality single shot chambered in 45-70. We chose this cartridge for its range and power level, and like the straight wall revolvers we talked about, it is quite easy to reload.

The Ruger Number One, Thompson Center line of single shots and even the reproduction Sharps rifles from Pedersoli, Cimarron, and others make great candidates.

(Ruger No. 1 single-shot with custom barrel with action open – photo credits Arthurrh)

As in the case with the semiauto handguns, we are not saying to discard your modern equipment, but having a few "Old Tech" designs on hand is just a safe bet.

Ammunition

As has been witnessed in the first half of the year 2013 firearms can become useless without a steady supply of ammunition. It does not take an act of war, alien invasion, zombie apocalypse, Congressional writ or Executive Order to halt the ammunition supply; the market can easily suffer as a result of speculation and panic buying.

When big box discount stores have to limit customer's purchases to 2 boxes a day it is a pretty good indication that it has gone beyond the warning stage.

Most shooters and those with a preparedness mindset could see events like these coming months if not years in advance and built their supply steadily. However, it was noticed that as the supply situation did not resolve within a reasonable amount of time, these prepared shooters had to resort to using ammunition that was saved for a rainy day with no signs for replenishment in sight.

Even dedicated reloaders of ammunition faced the same pitfalls as the companies who make ammunition also make reloading components. The major manufacturers saw their components going right back to their own production lines to feed the consumer demand for more ammunition.

When traditional methods of acquiring ammunition are not available, the shooter needs to think outside the box on occasion in order to ensure that their ammunition supply stays constant. With regard to reloading ammunition and casting or swaging bullets, it is essential to take every reasonable precaution suggested by the manufacturers involved. There is always an inherent danger involved, but this can be strongly minimized by practicing safe loading and handling procedures.

Again, we can look to the time of the Old West, when the art of reloading was born, but take advantages of modern machinery and methods at the same time. During our frontier days, reloading or even casting bullets was more often than not a necessity. Most black powder firearms came with a bullet mold to cast the appropriate sized bullet and prior to the era of cartridge firearms, powder was carried in metal flasks or powder horns.

Reloading Components

In the picture: Components of a modern bottleneck rifle cartridge. Top-to-bottom: Copper-jacketed bullet, smokeless powder granules, rimless brass case, Boxer primer (photo credits: Arthurrh)

If you were to read an article or a book on hand loading published in the past 100 years, the one statement that is constantly parroted is the great "savings" that comes with reloading. However, if the cost of brass, bullets, primers and powder was tabulated; this savings comes across as minimal, especially when factoring in the cost of dies, presses and other equipment. Over a long period of time the savings becomes more apparent, particularly when reloading the same cases repeatedly. As a business plan, many potential ammunition manufacturers have failed, even when purchasing components at wholesale or distributor prices. What is it that makes hand loading profitable or even preferable to reselling another manufacturer's ammunition?

The answer is in sourcing the components. We determined long ago that sourcing one or two components independently was the key to making a reloading business profitable, but this mentality can be applied to the shooter looking to produce their own ammunition.

The manufacture of modern primers and smokeless powder should not be attempted by the novice and should be handled by companies that adhere to strict quality control. For our purposes that leaves brass cases and bullets.

The Cartridge Case

Sourcing cartridge cases is the basic foundation of a reloading effort. It starts with the shooter saving their cases and perhaps obtaining cases from other sources. Without brass cases, there can be no ammunition.

Most cartridge cases are made of brass, although lacquered steel, zinc, aluminum, copper and even plastic can be used. Of all these materials, only brass cartridge cases are suitable for reloading.

Brass cartridge cases can be bought in wholesale lots, bartered for or collected from shooting ranges. When using range pickups, the hand loader needs to inspect for Berdan primers. This is an older type of primer mostly found in surplus ammunition from Europe and are evidenced by two flash holes inside the case as opposed to the single flash hole of the Boxer primer. Although technically they can be reloaded, they require specialized and expensive tooling to do so, as well as a supply of Berdan primers.

Additionally steel and aluminum cases cannot be reloaded and can cause damage to the shooter's reloading equipment if this is attempted. Aluminum cases mostly have a flat grey metallic color and are most commonly found with a "CCI Blazer" head stamp on the rim of the case. They can further be identified by their use of Berdan primers and their distinctive pair of flash holes inside the case. Steel cases typically have a dark green, black or even copper colored case to reflect an anti-corrosive coating on their exterior. Like aluminum cases they are most often found with Berdan primers.

Lastly, certain calibers will only sustain a certain amount of reloading depending on the firearm that has fired them. This is most notable in 40 S&W rounds fired in pistols with unsupported chambers (1st and 2nd Generation Glocks) or 223 or 308 ammunition fired from H&K or CETME rifles which use a fluted chamber to aid in extraction. These particular pieces of brass should be avoided at all costs and make good candidates for the scrap bucket as repeatedly resizing them will weaken the brass and will eventually result in catastrophic failure.

Processing Brass Cartridge Cases

In order to be an effective hand loader, one must inspect, sort and process the brass cases in order to ensure that the ammunition will be safe to load. Processing helps eliminate the Berdan primed cases, aluminum cases, steel cases and hopefully any cases of the incorrect caliber or that are not in their correct specifications.

While inspecting cases, the shooter should look for cracks in the neck and excessive bulges near the base. More than likely these cases will not resize properly and will need to be discarded to the scrap bucket.

When using brass that has been fired and collected from a shooting range it is advisable to clean and lube the cases. This can be done in a media tumbler with crushed walnut shell or dried corncob. Polishing chemicals can be added to speed up the process as well as special lubricants that will reduce wear and tear on the reloading equipment.

Depending on the equipment used, the brass can be de-primed at this time. This is usually done via a single stage reloading press and a de-capping pin. This step in the process resizes the case mouth as well.

Primer Pocket

The primer pocket is the part of the cartridge case where the primer is seated. Some types of military surplus brass will have an extra crimp to hold the primer in place. While processing brass for reloading, the crimp will need to be removed. In extreme cases the pocket will need to be de-burred or reamed so a new primer can be seated.

Bullets and Projectiles

Bullets are the one component that can most easily be made and stockpiled by any shooter of any skill level. Again, the prospective hand loader has choices instead of simply buying bullets or even the base material with which to cast them.

When it comes to store-bought bullets, the possibilities are seemingly endless. Leafing through a supplier's catalog or scrolling through a manufacturer's webpage can be overwhelming when it comes to choosing the correct bullet for a reloading project. Most manufacturers will list the weight of the bullet (typically in grains) and the profile of the bullet as well as the composition.

With the exception of specialty made bullets, most will be sold at a similar price point. The major cost will usually be the shipping charges (bullets in bulk can be heavy). An alternative to ordering from manufacturers, distributors or internet retailers that require shipping to the customer can be in the form of finding a local bullet manufacturer where the bullets can be picked up locally. If this does not seem to be an option, the enterprising hand loader can always make bullets at home.

The Cast Lead Bullet

The easiest type of bullet to make is the cast lead bullet. Lead bullets work best in handgun calibers (particularly revolvers) and rifle rounds loaded less than 1000 feet per second. Any bullet travelling faster than this will cause excessive leading in the barrel. This can be alleviated in certain calibers to a degree by using a gas check; which is a cup or disc made of a harder metal that is situated at the rear of the projectile.

Lead can be bought in lead ingots of the proper alloy for shooting or it can be found by digging up the berms of shooting areas; sourced from rivers, lakes and streams in the form of old fishing sinkers or

dive belts and obtained from tire shops in the form of old wheel weights. Most tire shops will be happy to give it away as they typically pay for disposal.

When lead known as bullet alloy is acquired it is actually a mixture of lead, tin and antimony. These additional elements aid in making the bullet harder than lead, by itself to reduce leaving lead deposits in the rifling of the barrel when a bullet is fired at a velocity greater than 1,000 feet per second. Recycled lead will not often have these properties.

Casting Bullets

Making cast bullets is simple in theory. The lead must be melted and poured into appropriate size molds for the caliber in question. However, lead is a toxic substance and must be handled and prepared carefully. With proper precautions this can be performed safely.

There are three essential pieces of equipment needed to cast bullets:

- ❖ Bullet mold
- ❖ Lead melting pot
- ❖ Ladle

Other equipment to have on hand includes a respirator, work gloves and an old metal spoon.

The Bullet Mold

It is paramount to research which bullet profile will work best in the firearm in question before investing in a mold. This can most easily be accomplished by the shooter purchasing factory ammunition with a lead projectile of a similar profile and trying it out in the firearm beforehand.

After determining which rounds work well, the goal will be to attempt to reproduce that load; the first step toward that goal will be to produce the bullet in question with the appropriate sized mold.

(Two bullet molds. The single cavity mold is open and empty. The double cavity mold is closed and contains two bullets – Photo Credits: Thewellman)

Bullet molds can be purchased for almost any caliber and different manufacturers will offer different patterns or profiles of different weights for each.

The Lead Melting Pot

A melting pot can be made using an old stock pot or cast iron pot. If the bullet caster has the means, a special purpose electric pot specifically made for melting lead can be purchased.

Lead melts at 600 to 621 degrees Fahrenheit. This means that the caster must be able to supply a heat source of that temperature. Because of the potential toxic fumes, the lead must be melted in a well-ventilated area, preferably outdoors. If the temperature gets hotter than 650 degrees, the potential for toxic fumes becomes even greater so a gauge of some type should be used to monitor this. The special purpose lead melting pots often have these gauges built in.

It is strongly advised to use a respirator and gloves while melting the lead.

The Ladle

The dipper or ladle is used to pour the molten lead from the pot into the mold. Some of the special purpose melting pots have a bottom spout to alleviate this. Some old time bullet casters prefer the ladle, even when they have a bottom spout because they believe the pour is more consistent.

The Melting Process

It can take 10 to 20 minutes for the lead to melt at the proper temperature.

If the caster is utilizing recycled lead, impurities will separate and rise to the surface. This will be in the form of dirt or even residual jacket material or lube with regard to recycled bullets. Recycled wheel weights may have rubber or other metal as a residue. The rubber and lube will burn off, but the metals and dirt will need to be sifted and removed from the lead pot before pouring it to cast by use of a metal spoon. These impurities will appear blackish in color and after removal may leave a trace color within the molten lead. These impurities should be placed in a metal container for disposal.

Wax shavings can be introduced to aid in fluxing out any remaining impurities. After stirring in the wax, the caster should scrape the bottom and sides of the melting pot to remove every last bit of these impurities before pouring into a mold. The final product should be a bright silver color.

The Casting Process

It is important to follow the manufacturer's instructions completely when using a bullet mold. Some will recommend heating the mold; some will recommend using a release agent, beforehand.

Whether the caster is filling the mold from a bottom spout or using the ladle, the molten lead needs to be poured directly into the hole on the top of the mold's sprue plate until there is a slight overflow (which is called sprue and how the plate gets its name). This will allow the mold cavity to fill properly as the lead cools.

The bullet will take its shape in about five to seven seconds. The caster can then rotate the sprue plate by tapping on it with a wooden dowel or a rubber or wood mallet. The sprue plate should cut the excess lead from the top and the open mold should release the bullet. The bullet may need to be tapped free of the mold by using the mallet again.

Your first bullets may have a crackled or wrinkled appearance due to the mold being too cool. Eventually the mold will achieve the proper temperature and the bullets will look fine. If they take on a frosted appearance it means the mold is getting too hot.

These newly formed bullets should be dropped into a towel, wooden box or in some instances, a pan of water to quench the bullets. The excess lead sprues can be added to the melting pot along with any flawed bullets and melted again to make new ones.

The bullets should be allowed to cool down and set for at least 24 hours before hand loading. In most cases the bullets will be ready to go at this point. If the bullets prove to be inaccurate, they may need to be resized to fit the firearm's bore. There are specialized motorized tools that can be bought for this purpose for under $1000 or the bullet caster can purchase a bullet sizing die of the appropriate diameter and mount it in a single stage reloading press in order to process several batches of properly sized bullets.

If you wish to size and lubricate the bullets, there is a specialized tool for this or the bullets may be lubricated individually. Spray lubricants can be applied or the caster may want to take another step and apply a coating.

Swaging Bullets

Bullet swaging is an alternative method of producing bullets at the individual level. It is mostly used by major ammunition manufacturers with expensive machinery and dedicated factories. Swaging utilizes pressure to form a bullet. As opposed to casting, no heat is needed and there is no requirement to melt the lead. Of course this negates the ability to use recycled materials such as dive weights, wheel weights, fishing lures or previously fired bullets, but it is the way to go if the hand loader wants to produce jacketed ammunition or specialized bullets such as a hollow based wad cutter. For making effective use of pre-existing materials, previously fired brass rim fire cases can be recycled and used as jacket material.

The pressure to swage a bullet is applied by means of either a hydraulic or hand-powered press. The press holds a die and a set of internal and external punches. The two punches apply force against the material from both ends of the die until it flows and takes on the actual shape of the die. When manufacturing a jacketed bullet, the lead core or wire is forced into the jacket material in the same manner.

Swaging can be performed in a home workshop using machinery made by companies such as Corbin. Most of the presses used for reloading can be used in the swaging process to swage the bullets, form bullet jackets from copper strip or tubing and make the lead wire, itself. Corbin offers dedicated swaging presses that can be easily converted to single stage reloading presses as well.

The initial set-up of a swaging operation is more costly than a basic casting venture, but can be more versatile, particularly if the end user has a greater need for jacketed ammunition for use in semiautomatic rifles and handguns. There is a reduced risk of exposure to toxic substances and the operation can be conducted "under the radar" with no one being the wiser to a manufacturing facility as they would with the smell of melting lead ingots. The end-user does not have to be concerned with fluctuations in the molding and casting process due to temperature, either.

After the initial cost of setting up the machinery, the cost of bullet production is essentially the same cost as the raw materials and the end result is usually a more accurate bullet as opposed to a cast bullet.

Machining Bullets

In some instances, bullets can be machined. Although it is not an ideal situation, it can be a method of last resort. We know several shooters of 338 Lapua Magnum and 50 BMG who have found it cheaper to turn out bullets for these rifles on a lathe or a screw machine. Some use bronze or copper and one uses steel in his 50 BMG rifle.

The problem with steel is that it quickly erodes the bore of the rifle; however the shooter in question maintains that he spends so little on reloading components that he finds it cheaper to replace the barrel after it is shot out.

The Final Word on Lead Bullets

Lead is a toxic substance that can cause health problems and birth defects. It is advisable to wear gloves whenever possible while handling it and strongly advised for reloaders to wash their hands with cold soapy water after handling it and before eating drinking or enjoying tobacco products.

HOW TO MAKE GUN POWDER
THE OLD FASHIONED WAY

- By Mike Searson -

"War is a terrible trade. But when the cause is just, the smell of gunpowder is sweet."

– Myles Standish

Would you believe that this powerful propellant, that has changed the world as we know it, was made as far back as 142 AD?

With that knowledge, how about the fact that it took nearly 1200 years for us to figure out how to use this technology in a gun. The history of this astounding substance is one that is inextricably tied to the human race. Imagine the great battles and wars tied to this simple mixture of sulfur, carbon and potassium nitrate. Mixed in the right ratios this mix becomes gunpowder.

We have just become such a dependent bunch that the process, to most of us, seems like some type of magic that only a Merlin could conjure up. So, I will lift the veil on gunpowder.

Gun Powder Formula:

- ❖ 75% Potassium Nitrate
- ❖ 15% Charcoal
- ❖ 10% Sulfur

Recipe For Homemade Gunpowder

Tools:

- ❖ Digital Ounces Scale
- ❖ 2 Glass or Plastic Mixings Containers
- ❖ Plastic spoon
- ❖ Blunt object for smashing potassium nitrite (I used the handle of a small tack hammer)
- ❖ Fine mesh sieve

Ingredients:

- ❖ Potassium Nitrate (Salt Peter) / Stump Remover
- ❖ Activated Charcoal
- ❖ Powdered Sulfur

Technique

A little safety first before we get into steps and instructions. Sulfur can kill you and the gas it gives off when burned can kill you. Potassium nitrite is no picnic either, it can damage your vision and poison you if ingested. Gunpowder is highly flammable/explosive and could cause you great physical harm.

- ❖ Wear eye protection
- ❖ Use gloves
- ❖ Use a dust mask
- ❖ Work in a well-ventilated area
- ❖ Most importantly use common sense

PROCEED WITH CAUTION!

Gather your ingredients and measure them based on the black powder formula above. Whether you are making 1lb or 10lb the breakdown will be the same 75% Potassium Nitrate, 15% Charcoal and 10% Sulfur.

Next mill or grind your saltpeter. Most recommend doing this in a ball mill but I wanted to do this all by hand to get an idea of how it would work without conveniences.

Once the potassium is ground add the measured charcoal and sulfur and begin to mix the ingredients thoroughly.

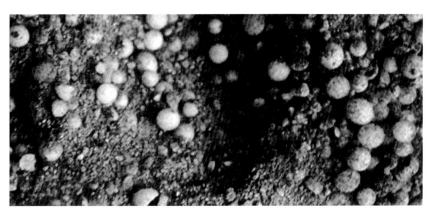

As you can see in the photo above the mix was not completely smooth so I ran it through a mesh sieve to remove and potassium nitrate that had not been ground fine enough. This process created a much finer powder and helped incorporate the three ingredients.

It worked so much better than hand mixing I just ran it through the sieve again. You can really see it becoming something at this point.

The sieve was crucial to this process if you are going to be doing it by hand. The finer the sieve the better.

I was very happy with the consistency achieved in such a short amount of time. This whole process may have taken 30 minutes. Most people recommend you run the ingredients in a ball mill for 12 hours! That said, their black powder is of a superior quality in comparison to what was created here by hand. Still, this stuff would get the job done.

This is how the final product looked like.

So, then I folded a small piece of paper in half and laid that on a rock before lighting it. Light this stuff from a distance with a torch or a long piece of paper. Especially the first time. You will not know how good your black powder is and you don't want to find out by having it scorch your face.

If you want to make it more powerful here are two great tips for powering up your gunpowder:

Add water to the mix and stir it into a paste then allow it to dry. This really gets the three powders to mingle thoroughly. Add (isopropyl) alcohol to the mix depending on batch size and this will make it really angry when the fire hits it.

Making gunpowder at home is one of those cheap and easy endeavors that will surprise you. It's also puts you in contact with a process that changed the course of history! Just be safe and smart as you are creating a highly combustible substance!

Smokeless Powder

After the discovery that burn rates of powder could be controlled by changing the granule size of the powder, Viellie and Nobel introduced smokeless powder to the world. This new powder did not have the corrosive or hydroscopic properties of black powder, and most importantly, it did not leave clouds of white smoke in its wake when a round was fired. Because of the higher pressure involved with smokeless powder, it should only be fired in modern firearms made after 1898 and never fired in firearms marked "For Black Powder Only."

OUR ANCESTORS' GUIDE TO ROOT CELLARS

- Theresa Anne DeMario -

"If you don't have a plan and leave your food choices to chance, chances are good that those choices will stink."

— Kristen Bentson

With the cost of food rising and the quality diminishing every year, root cellars are not a thing of the past. Nor are they just a way to prep for an uncertain future.

A well-tended root cellar will dramatically reduce your cost of living now, freeing up those much-needed funds for all those unperishable items that will make your life a little more comfortable when the time comes.

A root cellar is the perfect place to store the bounty of your summer garden, but it is also useful for those trips to the farmers' market when you find a particularly great deal on turnips but you know you won't eat that many before they shrivel up on the shelf of your pantry. When I think of a root cellar, I picture a space set in the side of a hill, lined with stone[25]. All year, it stays cool and damp—a glorious reprieve to escape to after a hot summer's day in the garden.

More commonly, root cellars are less exciting, with dirt floors and wooden shelves. These work too. In fact, when it comes to function, a cave, an unfinished basement, a bulkhead, or even a covered trench will get the job done.

History

The oldest examples of root cellars date back some 40,000 years ago in Australia. Incidentally, this is also when fermentation was discovered. People would grow copious amounts of yams and bury them to eat later.

Sometimes they would ferment, so alcoholic beverages became a happy byproduct of food storage. When you think about it, this is probably also how and why the wine cellar was invented. In fact,

---

[25] *"Philander Knox Root Cellar" by: Thomas, (CC BY-ND 2.0)*

we've unearthed underground storage from the Iron Ages, when it was common practice to bury immature wine.

However, root cellars as we understand them today—a convenient, walk-in food storage space—is a relatively young idea that dates back only to 17th century England. In the rest of the world, food preservation techniques, such as pickling, salting, and drying, excelled. A happy combination reached the Americas during colonization.

The Right Space for the Job

Like history has shown us, root cellaring is not necessarily the best choice for every environment, and even within the same climate, there are different kinds and ways to adapt a root cellar to your individual needs.

Climate

Depending on where you are, your root cellar needs to perform specific functions for you. If your climate is one of extremes, you need to take this into consideration.

If you are in the southern half of the country, you probably experience rather mild winters, and it may be difficult to maintain the low temperatures required for long-term storage of many things. Even though this is true, a well-built root cellar will probably keep cooler temperatures than you would otherwise get, and keeping the right humidity can bring the temperature down just low enough to suffice. If you are in a very dry and warm area, just go with it. Use the cellar to store your sun-dried bounty, nuts, and grains.

If your problem is a very cold environment and you are more worried about freezing your bounty, then you need to be sure to line your walls with extra insulation to keep the cold at bay.

A bare bulb hanging from the ceiling may give enough heat, but you'll need to cover root vegetables to keep them from sprouting. Ingenuity in rural building includes covered pits filled with composting manure.

The decomposition creates heat that in turn heats the root cellar by a few degrees. Remember that cold temperatures dry the air, so be sure to keep tubs of water to keep up the humidity.

Many things besides temperature can affect the type of root cellar[26] you use.

A big determining factor is the floor plan of your house. Another one is the lay of your land. If you have an older

---

[26] "Root Cellar" by: Jeff Wilson, (CC BY 2.0)

home with an unheated basement, then you've probably already got everything you need. Just pick a corner, set up shelves, and get started.

If you decide you want an outdoor root cellar, there are a couple of things to keep in mind before you start digging. If you are in the hard north, you may want to consider a root cellar that is easy to get to, like under your porch as opposed to one you may lose under the snow in the winter. Remember that you will have to make semi-regular visits there, so don't put it any farther away than you will feel like digging out to.

In most of the rest of the country, even if we get a little snow, we can situate our cellars a little farther away. I still caution about placing them too far off since you still have to go out there in the rain, wind, or snow.

If you have a good hill on your property, this makes for a great location for your root cellar. If not, you can dig straight down and top the entrance with a bulkhead door. Maybe create double doors to keep it safe from the elements.

Another thing to consider is that if your winters are especially mild with averages that hover well above 30°F, a root cellar may not keep your root vegetables as fresh as just leaving them in the ground over the winter.

The warm and dry produce should still be brought in and put up, however, so they don't rot.

What to Keep Where

If you find that you are indeed in the ideal location for a cold and damp root cellar, congratulations! You are ready to sever your ties to the corporate food machine. The bulk of your storage foods do best in this environment. Of course, there are exceptions. Some produce prefers a dry environment instead. A dual chamber root cellar with damp and dry rooms has more value than you can imagine.

If you can afford it, look into building a root cellar with both. Otherwise, a closed-in patio, unheated basement closet, or any space that gets cool enough but stays dry will work nicely.

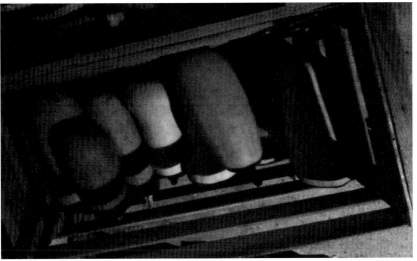

Keep these foods[27] cool and dry:

❖ Beans

_____

[27] *"Stored squash" by: espring4224, (CC BY 2.0)*

- ❖ Garlic and onions
- ❖ Pumpkins
- ❖ Squash
- ❖ Sweet potatoes
- ❖ Tomatoes

Creating the Ideal Conditions

Designating a space as your root cellar might be the easiest part of the job. Creating the perfect storage conditions within that space, however, takes thought and sometimes more than a little ingenuity.

Lighting

Many things will sprout or even deteriorate if exposed to light for too long. For this reason, your root cellar[28] should remain as dark as possible when not in use. For those times when you do need a light, you can get as fancy or as simple as you please.

As happy as you will find yourself while gazing at your bounty, a crystal chandelier may not seem so out of place. Most of us will opt for the single unshaded lightbulb though. If you don't have your root cellar wired, that shouldn't be a problem either. There are many battery-operated light fixtures on the market, and although I prefer good lighting to inspect my treasures by, a flashlight will get the job done.

Humidity

Have you ever brought beautiful produce home and put it in the fridge only to watch it wither and shrivel away into a nasty brown lump? Moisture moves. Water knows this. It's a cycle of condensation and evaporation that keeps it on the go at all times. It is constantly moving from the ground to the air and back again.

Much like people, your produce is mostly water. If left to its own devices, the water in your produce will soon leave its earthly shell to frolic in the air. The only way to prevent this is to convince the waters of your produce that the earth cycle is not over. The trick is

---

[28] *"Hylätty perunakellari" by: Janne, (CC BY-SA 2.0)*

to keep the humidity pretty high in your food storage area. As much as 90% to 95% humidity is ideal.

In some areas of the country, damp air is a matter of course. In dryer climates, keeping your root cellar damp does not have to be a big challenge. There are several tried and true methods you can utilize.

Dirt Floors

If you have earthen floors, you are good to go. You can sprinkle water on the floor, and it will evaporate and keep the air moist. If you reach down and touch your floor and it feels dry, it's time to water it again.

You may want to lay some gravel or wooden plank walkways to keep your feet from getting muddy.

Wet Cloth or Paper

You can hang wet linens in the room or cover your produce with damp (not dripping) pillowcases or burlap sacks.

Standing Water

Probably the most basic way to introduce moisture to a room is to simply put water there; wide, shallow pans have more surface area for more rapid evaporation, or a bucket in the corner might be enough if you don't want to check it that often.

Bury Your Treasure

If you've tried the methods above and simply cannot keep your humidity level high enough, try burying your roots in sand or sawdust. This prevents rapid dehydration and preserves them longer.

A Condensation Nightmare

There is that point when the air temperature changes and the cycle of evaporation becomes condensation. When this happens, you may be faced with a big, wet mess. That much moisture will spoil your precious foods and encourage mold, mildew, and general rot to take the room over. Save yourself this trouble. Buy a thermometer and a hygrometer, and check the levels regularly. Dew points vary according to atmospheric pressure, humidity, and temperature. If you can find out what is normal for your area, you can prevent a disaster by regulating these factors. Sometimes it's as simple as cracking the door for a day or so.

Ventilation

Some vegetables stink when they sit, and some fruits give off ethylene gas, which speeds the ripening and subsequent rot of your produce. This is why it's important to keep the air circulating.

Don't underestimate the value of good ventilation when setting up your root cellar. The key to good ventilation is to be sure it can be both monitored and controlled.

The easiest method is to simply put an intake vent close to the ground and an exhaust vent close to the ceiling. Then you just let the air circulate naturally—cool air sinks and heat rises. If you want to get fancy, you can install grates that open and close or a simple fan in the exhaust vent.

Don't be afraid to take advantage of your root cellar's ventilation system. Put cool keepers closer to the intake and gas producers closer to the exhaust. Remember to keep your crates off the floor, and leave plenty of space between them for the air to circulate.

Storage Ideas

Once you have your root cellar set up the way you want it, you are going to want to start storing food[29] in it right away. You most certainly can just start filling your shelves with loose produce if you

[29] "Root cellar storage" by: espring4224, (CC BY 2.0)

want to. There is nothing wrong with that straightforward kind of thinking.

But you will get more in and keep it in better shape with a little foresight and planning.

Whether you use crates, bushels, trays, or drawers is a matter of preference; each method has its merits. In fact, you may find yourself using all of them at some point or another. I've even heard of people using lidded trash cans to store their roots. A heavy duty one with a good lid would work marvelously. You could use old newspapers to layer in apples and you'd have a modern day apple barrel that would resist the most determined rodents.

In-Garden Storage

First of all, not only is it okay to leave your root harvest until the last minute but it's actually desirable. You will want to wait until the ground has cooled completely before you mulch over your garden. If you do it too soon, you will only trap the warmth and promote the composting and decay of your treasured roots.

You will need to harvest carrots before the temperature gets too low. They are damaged when frozen. However, kale is a champion fall green and will do fine out there through a few frosts. So will leeks and onions. Cabbage, cauliflower, and celery are pretty cold hardy as well.

Speaking of vegetables that tolerate the cold, turnips, parsnips, and horseradish actually improve when left in the ground for a light freeze. Just be sure that you don't let the conditions get to where your bounty is under a few feet of snow and you can't break ground any longer! It might prove best to go ahead and dig them up while you can and store them in containers outside for a while.

Insulation

While it's difficult to make absolutely sure that your root cellar stays the right temperature with the perfect amount of humidity, it is really easy to provide them with a little extra support via insulation. What sort of insulation you use is up to you.

Simply line the bottom of your container with an inch of insulation and layer in your produce, leaving a quarter inch between each layer.

Although root vegetables can touch each other slightly (as opposed to apples), you must be sure to leave one to three inches on each side between your produce and the container.

- ❖ Shredded paper
- ❖ Newspaper
- ❖ Sawdust
- ❖ Peat moss

Things That Do and Do Not Belong in Your Root Cellar

While the root cellar is the perfect place to store raw fresh produce, unless you have dual compartments, it is a terrible idea to store your canned or boxed foods there!

For one thing, your cans will rust, and it's never a good idea to keep dry food in humid conditions. For this reason, it's also a bad idea to store your dried beans and grains in your root cellar unless they are in airtight containers.

You can buy packs of silica online to absorb the moisture in these containers, or you can just find a cool, dry space in your house for them instead.

However, produce is far from the only thing that does well in the specific conditions of your root cellar. Think of how nice it would be to have a rack of wine bottles aging in there as well. Beers, ciders, and other bottled drinks[30] do equally well in the cool dark.

---

[30] *"Tin Top Antique Shop" by: Brandi Sims, (CC BY 2.0)*

Cured and smoked meats will last ages in a root cellar as long as the temperature stays below 40°. In fact, when it's that cool, you can store milk, cheeses, and other dairy in there too, with great success.

Proper Storage

Don't go tossing your green treasures on the shelf all willy-nilly. You worked hard to grow them and worked smart to get your root cellar together. Be sure that you do everything possible to ensure your harvest stays delicious for the cold season.

Cull the Crops

Harvest time is a time of plenty. It's a time to truly be thankful, no matter what the outside circumstances are. While you are harvesting, curing, and packing up the fruits of your labor, take a close look at each one. If there are any blemishes at all, cull them from the rest.

Don't throw them out though! Trim them and prepare them for dinner. Alternately, you can freeze, can, or dry them for later use. They just can't stay in the root cellar to spoil. This is the perfect time to invest in a make-ahead cookbook. These plan-ahead meal plans are gems at harvest time.

Put everything you need, including whatever blemished produce you culled, into individual meal bags, so it's all right there together when you need it.

Preparing Vegetables for Root Cellar Storage

Now that you have your harvest in front of you, you need to prepare it all for storage. You might be happy to learn that you do not have to wash it all before storage.

In fact, you really don't want to. No, really—unstop your sink. Do not, I repeat, do not wash those roots! If, by chance, you dug them up in wet weather and now they are all muddy, just let them sit out until they dry before putting them in the cellar. You can even pull them and leave them right there on the ground for a day or two. This will stimulate dormancy and lessen the likelihood of them sprouting.

Do not trim the roots off your tubers. You don't want any broken skin, because that's where the rot will start. Do trim the greens off of all of your root crops. Scrape the leaf area completely away because any tops left will only encourage decay in the roots around it.

Curing Winter Vegetables for Storage

Many vegetables must be cured before storage. Curing promotes a dormant state that prevents sprouting or rot. Onions and garlic should have their tops clipped with about an inch left behind. Leave these in the sun for a week before storing. Here's a tip: Pantyhose are the best way to store them. Simply fill the hose with the bulbs and hang them from a rack in a cool, dry room.

Pumpkins and winter squash need to sit out in the garden (or the porch, yard, wherever) for two full weeks before storing them. This gives them a chance to develop a good hard rind that will protect them throughout the winter. Then store them in a cool, dry place until you need them. The only exception is acorn squash. They don't store well, so don't bother. Just eat them and be happy.

Sweet potatoes also need to be cured. Keep them in a warm, damp space for a week to 10 days before moving them to storage.

Pests

Nothing will ruin your day faster than discovering pests in your root cellar. Whether it's mice, birds, or weevils, you don't want any visitors—period. In the case of pests, the old saying rings true today. The best offense is a good defense. Calk holes and cracks; play close attention to the area around your vents. While you're examining your vents, do you need to cover them with a mesh wire? Close the door and look for any rays of light. Check to see if you need to put a piece of weather stripping under the door.

Then, when the room is as secure as you can make it, look to your containers. If you already know you are going to have a pest problem, get containers with lids. Make sure the lids to grains are airtight, not just to avoid exposure to moisture but to prevent weevil infestations, and also keep all containers off the ground. You should do this anyway. The ground is often too moist for good storage, but it also makes it too convenient for pests to get to your food.

The best containers to prevent pests are plastic totes with lids, or like mentioned earlier, large, lidded trashcans would work like a charm.

Of course, tenacious rats will just chew through anything you put in their paths, so be sure to hide some good-quality rat traps in the corners, along the walls, or under your shelves.

Organization

Whether using totes or banana boxes, organizing your bounty so that you know what's stored where is almost as important as convenient access to everything.

Don't shove crates in front of or on top of other crates if you can avoid it. You need at least a small space between each for circulation. It also makes it nearly impossible to see what you have if they're too close.

Label everything. Don't be afraid. Go crazy with it. Label the shelves. Label the totes. Label the cat if you think it would help you to remember where everything is.

Put the variety, the date stored, and the projected use-by date so you know how much you need to cook before it goes bad.

Keep a notebook and pen on a shelf so that you can keep notes about the climate of your cellar; the keepability of the varieties you chose; and any interesting incidents or observations that may be important to you, your children, or whomever inherits your treasure room.

Tomatoes will not store for long, but if you still have tomatoes on the vine when the frost threatens, you can yank the whole plant and hang it upside down in your root cellar until the tomatoes ripen.

This method will lengthen the storage capacity of your long-keeping varieties for four to six months, no matter how you set it

Tips for Storage Success

1-Treat your produce like fine china. Bruises rot.
2-Inspect often. One bad apple really will spoil them all.
3- Harvest mature specimens.
4- Harvest while dry. Moisture encourages mold.
5- Wait until the latest possible date to harvest.
6- Choose long storing varieties.
7. Cool or cure promptly after harvest.

up, what you store there, or what ingenious thing you dream up to overcome the obstacles.

You are now well on your way to becoming as self-reliant as possible, and when you do, you will know deep down in your soul that you really are ready for anything, and that's just a great feeling!

Variety	Tempurature	Humidity	Shelf Life	Ethylene production
Apples	32-40°	90-95%	2-7 mo	high
notes: Choose good storage variety. Insulate so the apples do not touch.				
Beets	32°	98%	6-10 mo.	low
notes: Leave root tip and 1 inch greens on top				
cabbage	32°	98-100%	3-6 mo.	low
notes: Choose late varieties for storage. Red stores longer than green. Store near exhaust.				
carrots	32-34°	98-100%	6-10 mo.	low
notes: Remove tops. Best layered with sand or peat.				
celariac	32-35°	98-100%	6-8 mo.	low
notes: Store unwashed and unpeeled				
celery	32°	98-100%	2-3 mo.	low
notes: Keep small portion of roots attached				
garlic	32°	60-70%	3-4 mo.	low
notes: Leave unpeeled for storage				
kale	32°	95-98%	1 mo.	low
notes: Keep a close eye on your kale and use it up or freeze it if it starts to wilt				
kohlrabi	32°	95-100%	1-3 mo.	low
notes: With leaves, you have up to a month but topped plants store 2-3 mo.				
leeks	32°	95-100%	3-4 mo.	low
notes: Harvest whole and store upright in damp sand				
onion	32°	65-75%	6 mo.	low
notes: Must be cured prior to storage				
parsnip	32-34°	98%	1-2 mo.	low
notes: Remove tops. Best layered with sand or peat.				
pear	29-32°	90-95%	4-6 mo.	low when in cold storage
notes: wrap individually.				
potato	40-45°	60%	2-4 mo.	low
notes: must be cured prior to storage.				
radish	32-34°	98-100%	6-10 mo.	low
notes: store layered in sand near exhaust fan				
rhubarb	32°	95-100%	1 mo.	low
notes: store whole stalk with most of the leaf blades removed.				
rutabaga	32°	98-100%	4-8 mo.	low
notes: store layered in sand near exhaust fan.				
squash (winter)	50-55°	50-75%	2-3 mo.	low
notes: should be cured prior to storing except acorn squash which stores 1-2 mo.				
sweet potato	55-60°	90%	12 mo.	
notes: should be cured prior to storing and checked often for sprouting.				
turnip	33-36°	90-95	4-6 mo.	low
notes: store layered in sand near exhaust fan.				

387

GOOD OLD-FASHIONED COOKING ON AN OPEN FLAME

- By Theresa Anne DeMario -

"One of the very nicest things about life is the way we must regularly stop whatever it is we are doing and devote our attention to eating."

– Luciano Pavarotti

When planning for an uncertain future, the first thing you may want to do is build up your supply of food, but that act has little meaning if you have no way to cook it. Some serious preppers have already figured that problem out with alternative power sources and generators to run their electric ovens. The rest of us will have to make do with good old-fashioned cooking on an open fire.

Homemakers of the 18th and 19th century could turn out culinary masterpieces that were not only hardy but so good that the recipes have been copied, tweaked, and handed down, generation after generation, until they reached the modern era of convenience foods and microwaves. Now when you want a pie, all you have to do is pop down to the grocery and pick one up. Something was lost when we gave up the old ways of cooking. Let's face it—food tastes better when it's lovingly created and carefully tended.

If you want to not only survive disaster but to live and flourish, you'll want to learn to cook over an open flame like the pioneers did. With the right tools, heaps of patience, and just a little bit of practice, you'll be creating fire-roasted feasts like you've been doing it your whole life.

Cast Iron Cooking

Arguably, the most important investment you can make in your well-prepared survival kitchen is a good set of cast iron cookery [31]. Some people will tell you that aluminum is better.

The thought process there is that it is light and easy to carry. Many more think steel is the way to go. However, for durable, long-lasting cookware that will only get better the more you use it, nothing compares to cast iron. Cast iron can stand up to the heat of open fire cooking, and it is easy to maintain.

 Good cast iron is not cheap, but it's worth it to spend a little extra to get the good stuff. Otherwise, you may wind up sitting there, years after the economy has crashed and the supermarkets are empty, and you will be stuck with a flimsy pot that has a gaping hole in it where your cast iron ought to be.

---

[31] *"And G-D Said, Let There Be Brunch!", by: Ketzirah Lesser & Art Drauglis, (CC BY-SA 2.0)*

Care and Use

So now you know why you need cast iron. If you want your cast iron to be nonstick and easy to manage, there are a couple of things you ought to know.

Seasoning Your Cookery

If you buy your cast iron new, there will be instructions on how to season it included in the package. If you buy it used, chances are, it will already be seasoned.

Either way, seasoning it is pretty simple and should be done regularly anyway. To season your cast iron, simply slather it in oil and stick it over hot coals to cook the oils in.

Never Use Dish Soap

Good cast iron is coated in oil. Dish soap breaks down oil—that's how it cleans. You want to avoid this at all costs. If you do accidentally use soap on your cast iron, rinse it immediately and rinse it well, and then be prepared to re-season it.

If you are not careful, the soap will soak into the metal and taint your next meal. Instead of soap, use a good stiff brush or some steel wool. The settlers used wads of horsetail to scrub their pots and pans.

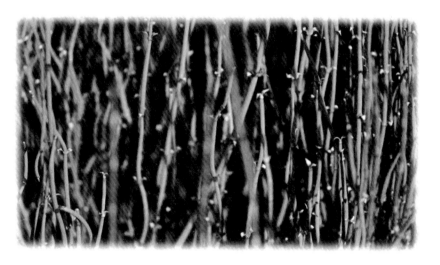

This highly fibrous plant[32] works well and can be found abundantly in damp places. In this day of disinfectants and germ phobia, it may seem counterintuitive to NOT use soap, but trust me, the temperatures needed to cook your meals are hot enough to kill any

---

[32] "Equisetum", by: Elnudomolesto, (CC BY 2.0)

potential germs, and a well-seasoned cast iron surface should be easy enough to clean without soap.

Iron Rusts

Because iron does rust, never leave it soaking in water or leave water in it. Even if you think it is well coated with oil, it will still rust. If you are not cooking with it, clean it, dry it, oil it down, and put it away. Stay in the habit of taking care of your cast iron. If cared for properly, it will last for generations.

No Fire

At the very least, don't leave an empty pot in the fire. It's tempting to just burn all the left-over food off, but cast iron can warp and even crack if left in a hot fire too long. For the same reason, don't put cold water in a hot pan. Again, take care of your cookery, and it will take care of you.

Companion Tools

If you are prepping a survival kitchen and you've got your cast iron, there are a few things you should think about packing with it. You'll need heavy pot holders because good cast iron is all metal, and those handles get HOT!

If you get a cast iron cooking pot, you'll want a metal hook to remove it from the fire. They also make heavy hooks to remove the lid of your pot that are sensibly called lid lifters. Tongs, spoons, spatulas, and other cooking utensils will also be necessary.

Roasting Meats

This is always what I think of when I think of outdoor cooking. Roasting trophy catches over an open fire is the epitome of frontier cuisine.

That said, if you've ever actually tried it, you'll know that it can be trickier than it looks. That's okay. Even roasting meat takes skill and know-how. The know-how you can get here. The skill will come with practice.

On a Spit

There is a wide variety of barbecue roasting spits available commercially, or if you're handy, you can make a good one without too much trouble. In the wild, you can use sticks to construct a spit above your fire. Be sure to leave enough of the spit stick on the end and out of the direct heat to be able to easily turn it.

You should always use a thermometer when checking your roast. And in some cases, doneness is a matter of taste. You can gauge about how much time you need to wait by these approximate times:

- ❖ lamb: 30 minutes per pound
- ❖ beef: 20 minutes per pound
- ❖ pork: 45 minutes per pound
- ❖ chicken: 30 minutes per pound
- ❖ venison: 20 minutes per pound

Treat small game like lamb, and expect 30 minutes per pound. Fish doesn't take as long, but because of the possibility of microscopic parasites, you want to be sure it's well done. When the skin peels off easily and the meat flakes, it should be ready to go.

On a String

This is one[33] of my favorite techniques for roasting smaller game, poultry, and dinner-sized roasts. If your cooking surface is your fireplace, then this is one cooking method you should familiarize yourself with immediately. It's easy, and the meat comes out perfect with very little fuss.

Choose the right-sized meats for this method. Don't choose heavy meats, or you'll break your string. You don't want big roasts either, because the center will still be raw as the outside burns. Chicken is perfect. Small game and reasonably-sized hunks of meat work too.

Once you've got your meat seasoned the way you like it, you will have to truss it up with some kitchen string. Either knot it well or go ahead and buy a set of trussing needles to attach the chicken to the string. You'll secure the legs and wings to the sides and hook it over the fire. If you have a wooden mantel, this is the perfect place to stick the hook. If you are outside, look for a good-sized branch or one of those iron hangers for hanging plants.

You'll want to place a drip pan under the meat to avoid any messes. As the string slowly unwinds, the chicken turns itself, making this a hassle-free dinner. Every now and then, twist the string back up,

---

[33] *"Roasting Chicken on a String 'a la Ficelle'", by: jules, (CC BY 2.0)*

and while you're at it, baste the meat and string occasionally to keep them moist.

It takes around an hour and a half to roast a chicken, but you should use a thermometer to make sure it's done.

Tips

Let that fire burn for more than an hour before you start cooking, feeding it when needed so that there are plenty of hot coals and less open flame. You want the meat close enough to get the heat without the fire touching it.

No matter what you are roasting, you want to try to shape the meat so that it is as even and cylindrical as possible. That way, it will be evenly cooked.

Dutch Oven Cooking

Even if you forgo the cast iron skillet or soup pot, you should have a Dutch oven. Not only can you bake in a Dutch oven but the body of the oven can be used for anything cooked in a pot, and the lid can be turned upside down to be used like a frying pan.

A Dutch oven can do it all and then some.

Cooking in a Dutch oven may take some getting used to. Figuring out how to get and keep the right temperature takes time and patience, but if you take that time and have the patience, you will be so happy with your Dutch oven dinners that you won't even miss the modern convenience kitchens at all.

Choosing a Dutch oven can be confusing. There are a lot of pots out there that call themselves Dutch ovens, but they won't do for what you need. So let's get some specifics down.

Your Dutch oven must be cast iron. It needs a tight-fitting lid that is either concave or at least flattish with a lip.

A Dutch oven with feet is best, but one without will do too, and the size only matters in the context of how many you are feeding and what you are making. I have a big family, so I have three: small, medium, and large. With these, I can cook a feast.

Care of your Dutch oven is the same as the care of the rest of your cast iron cookery. The same dos and don'ts apply.

The Right Temperature

Most guides and recipes[34] that you will find online today talk about Dutch oven heat in terms of how many coals it takes—so many coals on top and so many on the bottom. Let's face it—most of us preppers are not going to keep a store of charcoal on hand just to cook in our Dutch ovens. That's ridiculous.

People used Dutch ovens to cook with long before they could get standardized charcoal briquettes to barbecue with.

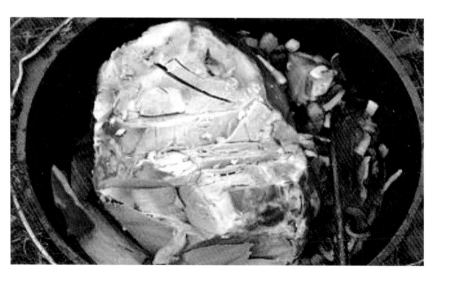

---

[34] "DSC_2275", by: Virginia State Parks, (CC BY 2.0)

The problem is that it's really hard to explain heat distribution in other terms, especially since different wood coals will hold heat differently.

Think in terms of equal space. You'll usually want to use as many coals as it would take to completely fill in the space below your oven. Distribute the coals according to the guidelines below. Adjust the amount as you see fit after you gain a little experience.

- ❖ **Roasting:** Using the starting amount of coals, put half on top and half on the bottom.
- ❖ **Baking:** Put a quarter of your coals on the bottom and three-fourths on the lid.
- ❖ **Simmering:** Place three-fourths of the coals on the bottom and a quarter on top.
- ❖ **Frying:** Put all your coals on the bottom.

Always space your wood coals evenly apart for the best results.

Companion Tools

There are plenty of good accessories to go with your Dutch oven. Depending on your cooking preferences, some of these will be more useful than others.

- ❖ Leather gloves and heavy potholders to handle a hot oven
- ❖ A lid lifter—a long metal hook used to remove the lid of your Dutch oven safely
- ❖ A small shovel to move coals around

- ❖ A trivet for baking or steaming in your Dutch oven to keep your food off the hot sides
- ❖ A cake pan to be placed on the trivet that is slightly smaller in diameter than your Dutch oven.
- ❖ —Long-handled tongs
- ❖ Other utensils that you would always use, such as spoons, spatula, etc.

Recipes Past and Future

These recipes were chosen to be easy and without too many exotic ingredients (sans spices—stock up on those!). With that in mind, enjoy the fruits of your labor. Your larder is well stocked, and your garden is growing well. You deserve a feast[35].

Colcannon

[35] "DSC_2292" , by: Virginia State Parks, (CC BY 2.0)

Colcannon is a traditional Irish dish that's brilliant for its simplicity. Boil a head of cabbage and twice as many potatoes as the size of the cabbage until good and soft. Chop and mash them together, and season with salt and pepper. Traditionally, colcannon was served with a healthy dollop of butter and cream.

Meat Pies

These are a beautiful way to use left-over meats, especially roasts, and stews.

Crust - Mix some flour with a little salt and some fat (butter, lard, whatever) until a stiff paste is formed. Use this to line the bottom of your pan, and if you have enough, cover the top of the pie too.

Filler - Use whatever meats and vegetables you have on hand. Thicken some broth or drippings with some cooked flour, mix it all together, and pour it over the crust.

You can cook this right in your Dutch oven if you like or in the cake pan if you want a smaller amount. Bake it for more than an hour, until everything inside is tender and the crust is crisp.

Turnovers are made with the same ingredients, but you make a big, flat crust and spoon some filling in the middle of one half. Fold the crust over and pinch it together, and then cook it on a frying pan. Turnovers were a popular meal to send off with working men and will hold up well for a day or so if prepared in advance.

Mock-mock Turtle Soup

Original mock turtle soup called for a calf's head to be boiled down for 8 hours. In this recipe, we'll use whatever meat we have on hand. Boil a pound or more of meat—with the bones, if you have them—for at least two hours. The water should be seasoned with bay leaves, parsley, marjoram, and basil (or just use what you've got). After two hours, toss in enough root vegetables, such as potatoes, turnips, and carrots, to feed your family. While this is cooking, take six hard-boiled egg yolks and mash them together with a little raw yolk and some flour to make a dough. Roll a dozen marble-sized balls, and toss them into the pot with a cup or two of red wine when the vegetables are almost tender.

Wassail

The Wassail bowl is a forgotten Christmas tradition. Even the old cookbooks refer to it as an old one. The spicy drink was ushered in with much ceremony and was often decorated with wreathes and ribbons. It would be a beautiful tradition to bring back when we find ourselves in need of a little reminding about the good things in life.

Many old recipes can be found for wassail. Depending on the cook, it might have beer, cider, or wine as the base. The spices vary too. Feel free to adapt and change the following recipe to include whatever you have on hand and to satisfy your own taste buds. This is as much a part of the tradition as drinking the wassail itself. In a small pot, boil the following:

- ❖ 1 tsp. cardamom
- ❖ 1 tsp. cloves
- ❖ 1 tsp. nutmeg
- ❖ 1 tsp. mace
- ❖ 1 tsp. ginger
- ❖ 1 tsp. cinnamon
- ❖ 1 tsp. coriander
- ❖ 1 cup of water

After about 20 minutes, pour this into a gallon of wine/beer or cider. Add 3 to 4 cups of sugar, and put in on the fire.

While it is cooking, prepare the wassail bowl by cracking a dozen eggs into it and beating them well. Add a cup of the warming wine to the eggs, and beat it in. Repeat this step three more times.

Then, when the wine begins to boil, take it off the heat and pour it gradually into the bowl, taking care to go slowly and stirring continuously. You need to stir briskly to form the froth that makes wassail so pretty.

Once you have it poured and frothed, serve it immediately. Roasted apple or a couple cups of raisins were commonly tossed in the wassail. A pint of brandy was also often used.

Apple Pie

Prepare a stiff paste for the crusts by mashing flour into fat (butter, lard, shortening). Line your well-oiled Dutch oven with the paste, reserving enough for the top. Make sure the crust is as even as possible. Roll the rest out to make your top crust. You only want your pie to be an inch or two thick, three max.

Peel, slice, and core your apples. You can parboil or stew them in a little water, but if they are very ripe, this is not necessary. Add cinnamon, sugar, and butter to taste.

Dampen the top of the crust in your Dutch oven, lay your top crust on top, and pinch them together. Cut a slit on top to vent, put the lid on your oven, and place it in the coals with a quarter of the coals on the bottom and the rest on top. It takes 45 minutes to an hour to bake a pie this way.

If you are using dried apples, reconstitute them and stew them for an hour or so before adding them to the pie. You should stew unripe apples as well.

Biscuits and Gravy

Start this recipe with a well-oiled Dutch oven. Preheat it, keeping all of the coals on the bottom to get it nice and hot. While it's heating up, mix the following together in a bowl:

- ❖ 2 c. flour
- ❖ 1 tsp. salt
- ❖ 1 Tbs. sugar
- ❖ 4 tsp. baking powder

Cut in 1/3 c. shortening. Then add ¼ c. milk. Mix only until everything is wet.

Spoon drop the biscuits into the Dutch oven, making sure they are evenly spaced, and put on the lid.

Now remove three-quarters of the coals from under the oven, taking care to even out the remaining coals. Put the coals you took out from under on top. Bake for 8–10 minutes or until golden on top. Remove and cover with a towel to keep warm.

Put the coals back under the oven, and add your meat. I like pork sausage, but my grandma sometimes used pork chops or just plain lard when there was no meat. Cook thoroughly. If you are using just a fat to make this gravy, and maybe even if you aren't, you'll want to season it with sage, thyme, and onion as well as salt and pepper.

Add ¼ c. of flour to the pot, and stir until well-cooked but not burnt. Then add 2 ½ c. milk and stir until thickened. Serve immediately by pouring over the biscuits on individual plates.

Easter Cake

Using this method, you can bake any and all of your favorite cake recipes in the Dutch oven. This Easter cake is an adaptation of a recipe found in the 1903 Boston Cooking School magazine. During times of crisis, there is little that says, "Everything is going to be okay," like a bit of cake. It seems cake just brightens the dreariest of days.

Preheat your Dutch oven using half and half for the coals. Use a trivet in your oven. If you don't have a trivet, similar-sized pebbles, marbles, or beads work well too.

Sift together 1 c. flour with 1 tsp. baking powder. Set aside. In a separate bowl, beat 4 egg whites until stiff. In yet another bowl, beat ½ c. soft butter with ½ c. sugar. Add 1 tsp. vanilla extract. Combine all ingredients, and mix well.

You need a cake pan that is smaller than your Dutch oven. A 9-inch cake pan and a 10-inch Dutch oven are ideal.

Pour your batter into a greased cake pan. Pour an inch of water into the bottom of your Dutch oven, and place the pan on the trivet. Leave the coals half and half for this recipe.

It takes 45 minutes to 1 hour for the cake to bake.

Porridge

There is not much that is more versatile than porridge. It can be made using oats, rice, buckwheat, or any other grain. It can even be made using peas.

Porridge was a traditional mid-day meal for peasants in Europe and the settlers of early America. This recipe makes the best breakfast porridge ever.

In the evening, dig a small ditch near your fire pit, and line it with hot coals. In your Dutch oven, combine 1 c. of rolled oats with 4 c. water and 2 c. milk. Add 1 c. applesauce and 1 cinnamon stick.

Put your Dutch oven in the pit, and cover it with more hot coals.

Then bury it with dirt. In the morning, uncover the Dutch oven, being especially careful not to dislodge the lid. Dust off the dirt and ash before serving (no one wants ashy porridge).

Stew

Like the porridge, stew is a favorite of days gone by. A stew is rather easy to make. In the morning, toss whatever meats and vegetables you have on hand in a pot along with your favorite seasonings, and cook it on a medium fire for most of the day.

An hour before it is to be eaten, thicken it with cooked flour, cornstarch, arrow root, mashed beans, or potatoes.

Serve and enjoy. Stews go particularly well with bread.

Bread

Making bread in a Dutch oven is easy! The trick is not to be too much of a bread snob. Use bread flour if you can get it. All-purpose works fine when you can't. Whole wheat works good too when you are using this method. Start the bread the day before you want to eat the loaf. Combine the following:

- ❖ 3 c. flour
- ❖ 1 tsp. yeast
- ❖ 1 tsp. salt
- ❖ 1 ½ c. water

In a large bowl, mix the ingredients until everything is wet, but don't worry too much about the lumps. Set the bowl aside in a warm, safe spot, and forget about it.

The next day, an hour before you want to bake your bread, preheat your well-oiled Dutch oven with half the coals on top and half on bottom. Meanwhile, turn your dough out onto a floured surface, and gently (DO NOT KNEAD) shape it into a roughly Dutch oven shape. You want it kind of evenly flat on top. If it rises too much, it will stick to your lid!

Move your coals back into baking position, and bake for 45 minutes.

HOW TO SHARPEN YOUR BLADES LIKE THE SAMURAI DID

- By James Walton –

"The Samurai always has to rise and move on, because new challenges will come."

– Lyoto Machida

Adominant warrior class of noblemen who also held some of the highest ranks in Japanese leadership, the samurai are legendary. There may have never been nor will there ever be a ruling class like the samurai ever again. This is not to say they were great heroes of history. In fact, their rule was part of one of the great military dictatorships of all time and the largest in Japanese history.

The Samurai swords were always worn and were considered an extension of their sole. They carried two swords each. A long sword, called the *katana* and short sword called the w*akizashi.* The swords are known for being some of the sharpest of their time and the technique is praised even today. It requires more than just a sharpener. It also takes lots of time, effort and skill.

Though they are rarely credited for such skills, samurais were also great archers. This was a part of their skill set and they utilized bows made from bamboo. The arrows were crafted from bamboo as well. This really got my attention in terms of creating bows. I had never considered bows and arrows from bamboo.

The samurai were also effective on horseback and in the 13th Century they fought off two Mongol invasions. This is a credit not just to the skill of the samurai but also to the resiliency.

Unfortunately, in the late 1800s the Samurai were abolished and the wearing of sword was forbidden soon after. It became a right for only active military personnel.

Of course, the traditions of the samurai live on in things like movies, ujitsu and other practices. We are going to discuss one such technique in this chapter. Though we do not carry swords today many of us have several blades in our EDC or fixed blade knives in our survival kits. These blades can be run across a sharpener to achieve a decent edge. I want to explore the process of sharpening like a samurai and creating a crafted razor edge.

The Samurai Sharpening Kit:

- ❖ At least two whet stones of different grains (I use a double sided)
- ❖ A piece of high grit sandpaper
- ❖ Polishing oil or mineral oil
- ❖ A ball of wax

We are going to use a standard military issued, fixed blade knife. As you can see it needs some work.

The traditional samurai sword is usually fixed in jigs during the sharpening process. For such small blades, we are going leave the stones stationary.

Soaking Your Stones

To use the wet stones properly you need to soak them for at least 20 minutes. This will allow the water to permeate.

It will be this water and the coarse grain that allows the knife to slide easily over the stone. I like to pour some water directly on the stone as well for lubrication.

Get a Grip

Depending on the size of your blade and handle you may want to bolster your grip. This may seem important for large blades like katanas but it can also be very important when sharpening small blades.

Theses knives usually have small handles that can be tough to bear down on. Don't slip and cut yourself!

Follow the Given Path

Before you begin sharpening you should observe the blade and take not of its natural curvature.

Your movements over the stone must match the proper angle and follow the curve of the blade as well. Remember, any part of the blade that doesn't touch the stone will not be sharpened.

Shitagi Togi

This is the first stage of sharpening and the coarsest stone you have should be used first. This is the portion of sharpening is for refining the once impressive shape of a worn blade.

You can also use this coarse stone to remove any nicks and grooves.

100 Strokes

Work each stone for 100 strokes on each side of the blade. After you have done this move to the less coarse stone. It takes a lot to bring back the razor edge by hand.

Pay attention to each stroke and follow that natural path of the blade.

Shiaji Togi

This is the point when you will utilize the fine grit sandpaper to really bring out the tempering line. You will work the sandpaper back and for the to define this tempering line.

On smaller knives this will be a challenge and you should hold the sandpaper with a cloth so if the blade cuts through it doesn't cut you in the process.

Polish

Use your sharpening oil and the residual grit from the process to polish the whole blade. My blade will require lots of polishing because it is pretty beat-up. You will see the payoff in the end.

Finish

Buff your blade with a ball of wax to finish the blade and wipe the entire knife down removing any residual dirt. After some demanding work this blade was brought back from the dead. I am

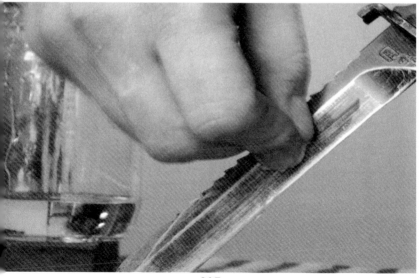

very happy with the blade achieved and the condition of the knife. The look has improved from the polishing as well.

Sharpening knives is one of those tasks that struggles against the tide of technology and time. Though, if you set aside the time to do an excellent job it's an entrancing and rewarding process.

HOW TO WAX CHEESE

- By Arminius -

"Knowledge is the key to survival, the real beauty of that is that it doesn't weigh anything."

— Ray Mears

Do you want to always have cheese on hand and not have to bother about going to the grocery store all the time? Well, waxing cheese is your answer because this is the best method to preserve it (and age it) for the long term.

In addition, wax protects the cheese from bacteria and mold. It also keeps it moisturized and reduces the time you have to spend working on the cheese.

Waxing cheese is the easiest and best thing you can do to take your love for making and aging cheese at home to the next level.

Ingredients

- ❖ Cheese (Ideally, permit the cheese to produce a bare, yellowish coating by being left unsealed on a stand in a cool area for some weeks.)
- ❖ Beeswax

❖ Honey to give the cheese an interesting taste. For 7 oz of cheese, I used a teaspoon of honey. (optional)

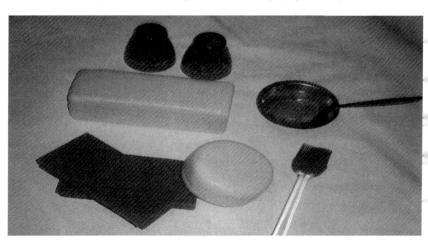

Melting the Wax

Melting the wax is as simple as melting any other material. You wil just need a heat source and a pot (preferably an old one since

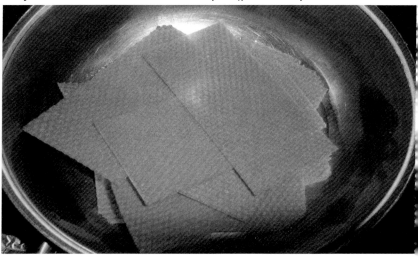

cleaning it will prove to be quite difficult).

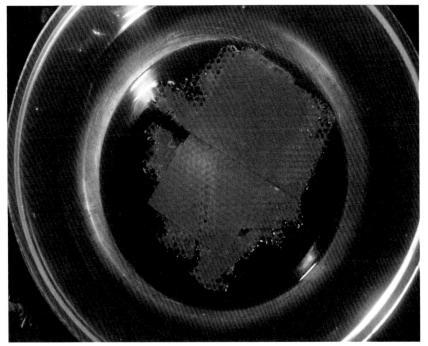

Warning: Molten wax is flammable, so make sure you check it regularly during the melting process.

Adding the Honey (Optional)

After the resin has melted, you need to take it off the stove and add the honey. Stir the mixture for five minutes so the honey dissolves completely and incorporates into the wax.

After that, leave it to rest for another five minutes to cool down enough so that you can handle it.

You can speed up the process by stirring it.

Brushing the Cheese/Dipping the Cheese

Before you start doing any of it, you need to choose your method. You can brush the cheese, and this will result in a more even wax. It also requires smaller quantities of wax 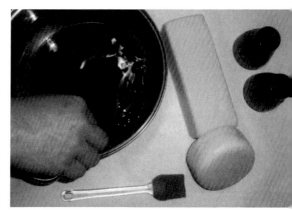 because you'll only need as much as the brush's length (to be dipped in).

Or you can dip the cheese, which is my method of choice because it kills off any mold spores that might still be on the cheese while preventing any further mold from growing.

Another advantage is that you won't have to trouble yourself with cleaning up a brush, but you will need to be very cautious with the heated wax since it can easily burn your hand.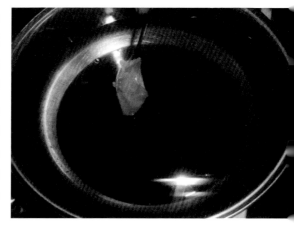

Dip the cheese into the wax, and leave it to rest for three seconds; then rotate it to the other side.

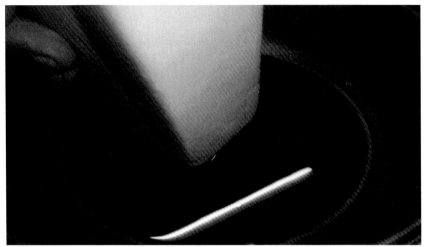

After that, take the initial portion of cheese and cover the unwaxed end. One light coat is better than a dense layer.

Let the wax solidify on the cheese, and repeat the same with the other parts of the cheese. Be certain to fill any air scopes to inhibit mold germination.

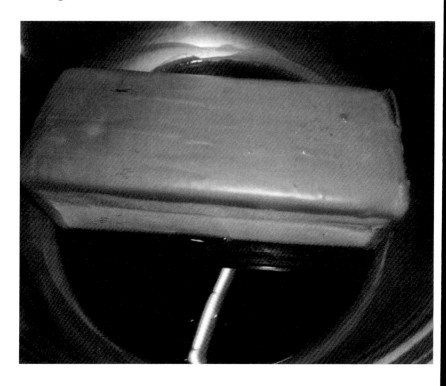

I would recommend doing this with bare hands, even though there's a risk of burning your fingers. It will give you a better grip when rotating the cheese. Repeat the above moves to join the second layer of wax to every part of the cheese.

And there you go—the finished product is done. Place it onto two glasses so it can dry faster.

The glasses are also necessary if you're brushing so that you have a good reach over the cheese, and I would recommend placing

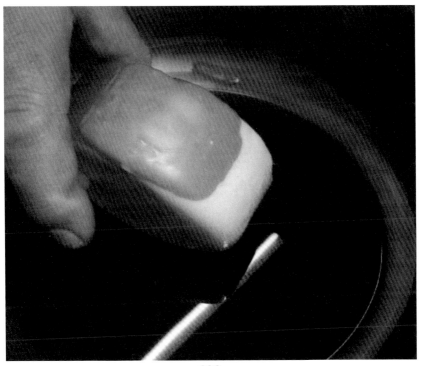

something (aluminum foil is best) under the glasses so you don't get the place messy.

After that, I did the same with a round cheese. I dipped it into the wax and slowly turned it around so I could get the entire circle. If you're doing multiple pieces of cheese, you might need to put the wax back onto the stove for a few seconds. This way it will be hot enough for the dipping.

After finishing up with this piece, place it onto the glass and let it sit for a few seconds; it cools off pretty fast, so you won't need to wait for long.

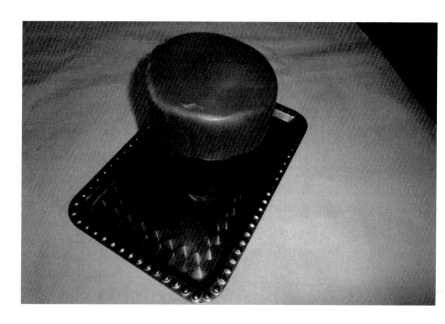

Collect all the wax that was left, and store it to use it at any time.

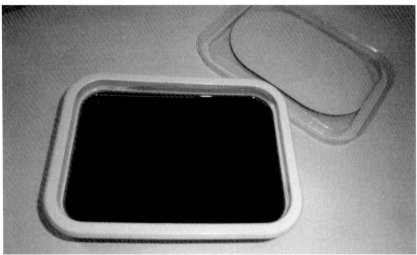

When you start eating your waxed cheese, you can seal the remaining chunks with some melted wax.

Cheese waxing is an easy and quick way to protect your cheese from anything that would slow down the process of aging it. The

entire process took me one to two hours to complete, but it was worth it! Your cheese will age beautifully and safely.

Essential Reminders

- ❖ When you discern any holes in your cheese later, you can just go back and add more heated wax to those points.
- ❖ The wax is always reusable. Therefore, you can eat your cheese and then learn how to preserve the wax for later purposes.
- ❖ Whenever you free your cheese and see spots of mold wherever the wax fractured and air leaked inside, simply chop off the ruined area. The remainder of the cheese will always be exquisite.
- ❖ Cheese will age over a season, so do not be shocked when your cheese tastes strange when you save it for an extended period. It should taste even better!
- ❖ You may also pre-cover your cheese using a cheese cloth. It difficult to use the already waxed cheese later since it was difficult to tear off a single sheet of the cheese cloth. I always put the wax on every bit of the cheese that we are not utilizing and seal up the free end using the wax of the pieces we used.

That is all there is to it! It is truly a relaxing routine and will make you feel great knowing that you have a great stock of cheese available and waiting for you!

HOW TO MAKE A WILD LETTUCE EXTRACT

-By Claude Davis-

"Don't find a fault, find a remedy"
Henry Ford

Wild Lettuce (One of The Best Natural Painkillers)

Wild Lettuce has been used by many people in place of addictive prescription pain medicine. It is also called opium lettuce.

The reason it's referred to as opium lettuce, is due to the pain relieving and sedative effects that it has been known to produce through a white substance found in the stem and leaves.

428

This milky substance is called lactucarium. And, while it doesn't contain any opiates, it has similar side effects when used – it acts directly on the central nervous system (CNS) to lessen the feeling of pain, just like opium and morphine.

Back in the 19th century, wild lettuce was already being used by some as a substitute to opium. But, it was in the 70's that it started to gain significant popularity by those wanting a more natural remedy. Individuals were starting to use it for both pain relief, as well as recreational purpose. In the earlier days, people using wild lettuce prepared it a couple different ways. One way was to cook the plant in a pan of water and sugar mix, until it reduced to a thick syrup-like consistency. While this was an effective form, it was quite bitter even with the sugar added. The most common form however, was drying the stem and leaves to use as an herbal tea.

The first thing you should do is to grind 50-150 leaves in a blender, but not very thinly, only for just a few seconds.
Place the ground leaves into a wide pot and add just enough water to cover them.

Now place the pot on the stove at low heat for 3-4 hours. Do not let it boil, because you'll destroy all the good stuff in it. Stir every 15 minutes until the water gets a dark brown color.

Now pour the substance while still hot into another pot through a strainer. Almost none or very little plant material should get through it.

Try to squeeze as much water as you can while the plant is in the strainer. This solution contains all the core elements of Wild Lettuce, especially the pain killing essence. But it's not concentrated enough. Yet.

So, in order to obtain this essence, you should warm it over low heat again until the water is vaporized, (while stirring) basically dehydrating the solution until it becomes a paste.

Be careful at the end when there is little water left, you should not burn the extract at bottom of the pot. What you should have now is pure Wild Lettuce Extract. You can now pour it in a small glass container and put it in your medicinal cabinet for when you'll need it.

Dose

The appropriate dose of wild lettuce depends on several factors such as the user's age, health, and several other conditions. At this time there is not enough scientific information to determine an appropriate range of doses for wild lettuce since this plant has only recently been rediscovered as a powerful remedy. But, the general 'customary' dosage goes like this:

Take 1 to 2 teaspoons in a cup of warm water. The effects of ingesting Wild Lettuce tincture are similar to opium, although no opiates are present in the plant. Effects are felt quickly but do not last long — between half an hour to a couple of hours.

OR

You can use 6-12 drops in juice or water, under the tongue or as desired.

May be taken 3 times daily. Shake well. Store in cool dark place. Keep out of reach of children.

Do NOT take more than 60 drops of tincture per day.